Terrorism and Militancy

TERRORISM AND MILITANCY

A Case Study of Political Development in Punjab

RACHANA KAUSHAL

KALINGA PUBLICATIONS
DELHI
1999

Terrorism and Militancy

ISBN: 81-85163-14-6

Rs. 295.00
$ 60.00
£ 30.00

Published by
Smt. Hem Lata,
Kalinga Publications
10A, Pocket I, Mayur Vihar, Delhi-110091

Laser Typeset by
Flash Photocomposers
37, Wazirpur Commercial Complex,
Delhi-110052 • Tel.: 7249527

Printed by
Shobi Offset Press
Kucha Chelan, Daryaganj
New Delhi-110002

Contents

Preface

The political system of almost all the developing countries are suffering from the crises of governability either due to the inability of the system to meet out the ever increasing demands of different groups or the inability of the ruling class to pay due respect to the demands of individuals, social, religious and ethnic groups which comprise the state. Minorities in most cases rise up against the governments of the countries in which they are living largely due to their dissatisfaction with their respective governments, leading to political struggle and internal instability. The experience of India in this respect is not different from other developing countries. Rather it has experienced a number of internal turmoil and disturbances which are still continuing in some parts of the country, even after 50 years of its independence.

This study, 'Terrorism and Militancy : A Case Study of Political Development in Punjab' deals with the rise of militancy and its consequences on the political development in Punjab and vice-versa. It analyses how militancy has hampered the functioning of democratic process and institutions and how politics of power contributed to militancy and terrorism in the state.

The study covers the account of the problem, genesis of problem, role played by history in giving rise to militancy, other factors responsible for violence and de-democratisation in the state, the use of religion as tool for political expediency and how the grievances of minorities are given communal overtones by the political elits to grab and sustain their control over power, the strategy of the government in dealing with the problem and the co-relation between militancy and political development i.e. how militancy, terrorism have hampered the functioning of democratic and secular norms of the nation and the role of politics in igniting the feelings of alienation and escalating them to the extent of terrorist and secessionist activities.

Though the terrorism in Punjab seems to have died down but the fact is that it is continuing in one way or the other putting a question mark on the governability and administrativeness of Indian state system. The study also suggests some ways to deal with such problems being faced by Indian nation.

This study is based on the published sources. It made use of different published sources like books, articles published in research journals and the news papers. Despite the generous help of so many, some discrepancies, however, could not be easily avoided. I, therefore, alone shoulder the responsibility for the deficiencies of argument in this study.

Acknowledgement

I wish to acknowledge my profound debt of gratitude to my teacher Prof. Iqbal Khanam for the encouragement, cooperation, and the invaluable suggestions given to me by her from time to time during the completion of this study. The knowledge she bestowed on me really helped me in understanding and analysing the Punjab problem resulting into the completion of this study.

I owe my deepest sense of gratitude to my respected teachers Prof. T.A. Nizami, Chairman, Department of Political Science, Prof. M.A. Kishore and Dr. B. Rahmatullah whose academic cooperation always encouraged and sustained my interest in this academic endeavour. I am also grateful to all other teachers of the Department of Political Science who provided all the help to me whenever I approached them.

I am also deeply beholden to my father, mother and my loving brothers who extended every help and cooperation to me. I shall be failing in my duty if I do not record my deep sense of indebtedness to my father-in-law, mother-in-law and my husband Mr. Sudhakar Sharma.

My gratitude also goes to all my friends and colleagues who rendered all needed help towards the completion of this study. I also acknowledge my thanks to the staff of Maulana Azad Library, A.M.U. Aligarh, IDSA Library, New Delhi, Seminar Library of the Centre for Strategic Studies, A.M.U., Aligarh. I beg to be excused for not mentioning the names of every one who also helped and cooperated me in this study.

Ms. Rachana Kaushal

1

Introduction

The political systems of the developing countries are facing a major crisis of governability in view of ever increasing demand loads on the polity. The term governability refers to the integrative capacity of the political system to produce desired results and also to maintain the various contradictions (socio-economic and political) operating in the system/society. In other words it refers to the enhanced capacity, especially of the administrative structure of the state to implement its policies and programme. In contrast to this definition, the polity of most of the developing countries, over the years, have witnessed the gradual erosion of this capacity to deliver the goods. The logic of democracy and the rising political consciousness among the deprived section of population, further sharpening the pace of demands of the polity and as a result polity is increasingly loosing its efficiency to sustain overloads, leading to the process of disintegration and in turn becoming vulnerable to all kinds of anti-democratic forces, which have/are producing crisis of governability amongst almost all Afro-Asian countries.

These polities are undergoing a process of de-institutionalization or dis-integration instead of political development, paving way for 'legitimacy crisis' of the political system.

The 'legitimacy crisis' which is the result of the erosion of capacity of the political system to deliver the goods (material resources, equality of opportunity and social justice) result in multidimensional violence — both physical as well as cognitive, can be seen in such form as communal riots, ethnic conflicts, group clashes, terrorism and other socio-economic as well as clandestine warfares.

This study basically concentrates on the problem of terrorism in a particular state of India which is undergoing or has undergone the above mentioned experiences. The main objective of its study is to understand and analyse the problem of terrorism in Punjab, its causes and consequences, the governmental strategy to tackle the problem, with special reference to political development in the state i.e. how militancy has hampered the functioning of democratic process and institutions and the impact of terrorism on the accepted democratic and secular norms of the nation as well as the role of politics in igniting the ongoing feelings of alienation and escalating them to the extent of terrorist and secessionist activities. Thus carrying a potential threat to the unity, integrity and security of the nation.

It seems that heterogenous societies (especially developing) are more prone to threats from inside rather than outside. With this new dimension of security, the concept need a reinterpretation. Security as such has undergone metamorphism. Since 1945 onwards, chiefly in reference to developing world. As most of the post-Second World War conflicts in the developing world are endogenous rather than exogenous, security can not be conceived in terms of physical protection from external military threat only. Traditional distinction between international and domestic conflict is meaningless when domestic ethnic and communal conflicts and the weak legitimacy of ruling elites is the chief source of instability and insecurity. Thus, a re-defined concept of security relates national security not only to external threats but also to domestic threats, instability of vulnerability or things necessary for promoting, maintaining security and development of the people.

Thus, while 'state security' refers only to 'territorial security', 'national security' is a much broader term. It stretches right from legitimacy and stability of governing elite to the protection of core national values which enjoy the consensus of entire nation. That basic structure on which rests the entire socio-economic, political and value system has to be preserved at any cost, which of course, require certain conducive domestic as well as global conditions. But this does not happen always. Most of the developing countries are either lacking in those 'conducive conditions' or they may be disturbed by the factors that are not only cross-border in origin but also emerge within the border.

Since security has political, economic, psychological, social as well as military dimensions causes may well be treated in the political-economy of the nation. Poverty, illiteracy, unemployment, natural disaster (may be due to man-made factors) loss of domestic cohesion as a result of ethnic or communal confrontation, intolerant and rigid attitude on the part of many or a particular section of society or the governing elite, perception of being neglected or the feeling of alienation from national politico-economic mainstream (whether genuine or not) exploitation of this feeling by political leaders/parties/transnational agencies/vested interest, which of course comes later on—all these factors carry immense potential to endanger stability and security of any nation.

In addition to all the above factors, equally strong threats to the security are instability of policy makers, lack of credibility on the part of governing elite, faulty strategy, ineffective handling, inability of policy makers to properly and timely identify and evaluate security threats.

Almost all the developing countries are equally vulnerable to the above mentioned (factors-related) potential threats to their security because of delicate, social fabric (on account of their heterogeneous nature) and the lack of a strong economic infrastructure. Most of the developing countries adopted the 'Western' model of political development without the required economic and social base. While western societies first took up the task of building up economic, technological and organisational infrastructure and the issues of legitimacy and economic and intellectual resources were built up before they broadened their political base to include mass functions, the non-western societies lacked this phenomenon. Neither the pre-requisite economic and intellectual platform was built nor enough of time consideration was given. Instead developing countries directly switched over to the process of broadening their political base without going in for economic, technological and intellectual infrastructure which has become a constant source of insecurity/alienation or a feeling of that kind posing threat to the national security and solidarity.

A brief analysis of the problem of militancy/terrorism in Indian states of Punjab, JK, N.E. reveal some common factors responsible for the rise of militancy in these areas :-

1. Economic factors — in the form of poverty, unemployment of the majority, lack of industrialisation, lop sided development.
2. Political factors — a feeling of neglect and lack of due share in the national power/governing power for example Punjab in the post-Green Revolution era

experienced a rising demand on the part of rich peasantry in the governance of the country and a tussle for political power began between National and Regional bourgeoisie.

3. Neglect of genuine demands — for example in Punjab, the demand for statehood, recognition of Punjabi language, distribution of river water.
4. Myopic national elite.
5. Lack of credibility on the part of political elite.
6. Faulty strategy — ineffective handling and inability of policy makers to properly and timely identify and evaluate security threats.
7. Deliberately creating or giving fuel to minor local issues and projecting them as gigantic national problems for political expediency.

Among all of them or most of these factors have been responsible for the rise of militancy in these states with such demands, ranging from autonomy, statehood to secession. Since India is a heterogeneous society—an abode of multiple— religious, regional, caste, ethnic and tribal identities which are highly sensitive issues and are exploited by the vested interest for political bargain. In Punjab Sikh vs. Hindu, in JK Muslims vs. Hindus especially Kashmiri Pandits, in N.E. Inter-Tribal or natives vs. plain immigrants — have been deliberately made an issue, throwing the genuine demands of employment, poverty eradication and education behind the scene.

The concept of militancy like terrorism is the subject matter of debate and discussion among scholars for simple reason that it has been used in various context and connections. It is frequently used interchangeably with term like terrorism, insurgency, low-intensity conflict. The violence in Kashmir is described as militancy whereas the same kind of violence in Punjab is termed as terrorism. Such kind of descriptions creates problems for clearly understanding the concept of militancy.

The term, militancy owes its derivation to word militare which means to serve as soldier. It also means the exaltation of force or reliance on it. It also refers to the readyness of an individual, group or community to take strong, harsh or violent action. Militant is one who is combative, who is aggressively active, always ready to take extreme action to demonstrate his opposition. Such a general description defies the clear-cut area of its scope. However, militancy refers to the combative, pugnacious tendencies of an individual, group or community. A militant could be a terrorist, a guerrilla, an insurgent, but not necessarily a terrorist will be a militant.

To begin with, 'Terrorism' is a brutal, undeclared, clandestine and lethal form of unconventional warfare.[1] Terrorism like other forms of unconventional warfare is the weapon of militarily weak, short of confronting the enemy conventionally in open combatment.[2] In fact, it is consistent with the essence of classical military strategy, the efficacious use of force to achieve a desired policy.[3] Terrorism, in other sense, can also be defined as a psychological warfare because it publicizes the terrorist's political cause, demonstrates their capabilities, disheartens enemy, discourages allies. It is a threat of violence or an act or series of acts of violence effected through surreptious means by an individual, and organisation or a group of people to further his or their political goals. The target of their attack are generally the innocent people and those in authority. Their strategies are based on alertness, mobility and attack. Though no mass support is necessary either for its emergence or its continuation but their tactics alienate masses from the legitimate system. The strategy of terrorism is such that it achieves its goal not through its acts of violence but through the response to its acts. In any other warfare violence is the beginning and its consequences are the end of it. For terrorism, however, the consequences of the violence themselves are merely a step towards the achievement of its objectives. The acts of violence in Punjab like indiscriminate killing of innocent people, bomb blasts at public places, in state transportations, kidnapping of prominent personalities etc. were directed to exercise pressure on the governmental machinery to succumb to the genuine/ingenuine demands of terrorists. The objectives of this form of warfare are manifold like revolution; changing of the entire system; dismemberment; autonomy; change of a particular government or change in a particular policy of a government.

Terrorism has been a serious problem for the security of nations. It creates such a mess that a nation finds very hard to let itself out. It has created a dilemma as how to defend native institutions and various interests against the threats of terrorism while preserving their essential character, popular support and willing compliance.[4] It has become a clear and dangerous threat to the normal and democratic life of the nations. It has made the democratic politics almost impossible. The election boycott of Sri Lanka, and El Salvadoor are the examples where it has destroyed the ground for any compromise,[5] or to take the example of the state under study, Punjab where militancy brought down the democratic process to a hault. It also created a climate of bitterness and hatred, poisoned the relations between different ethnic/religious/caste groups.

Terrorism has almost globalised itself. The dramatic value of terrorism during the past decade and its concomitant political and psychological impacts have produced a crisis of near global proportions.[6] Especially, developing countries with politically unstable systems, economically deprived and poverty striken masses, provide fertile ground of the eruption of this kind of uncoventional warfare. Terrorism has proved to be one of the major cause of instability in many developing countries. India is one of them with plural, heterogenic social fabric, widespread economic disparities regional as well as intra-regional, desire for greater power share, perceived threat to the identity culture and religion by the minorities provide favourable breeding ground for such kind of violent group/ethnic/communal clashes. Post-independent India faced insurgency, terrorism, militancy, naxalism in areas like North East, interior south, Punjab and Kashmir. In North East and some other parts of our country the situation is not yet peaceful.

In fact, the developing countries, including India are desperately struggling to maintain and defend their national and territorial integrity against clandestine warfares like terrorism.

In the case of India, democratic process has negatively operated to weaken its capacity of crisis management. The insensitivity and unrepresentative character of dysfunctional democratic institutions has further distorted the articulation of pressure politics of the bargain-counters. The diminishing charisma of regional and national leaders has changed the basic character of public protests and agitations in India. Deteriorating faith and confidence of people in democratic, peaceful and legal methods of bringing changes in our society is paving way for rising 'Cult of violence' which, if not checked properly, will ultimately destroy the tenuous civic order that exists today.[7]

The sovereign identity of India like many of the newly independent Afro-Asian nations fore-warrants a concept of territorial integrity and its sacredness. Whether it is India or any other developing country, heart of the problem is to preserve the national borders, integrity both from internal and external dimensions of threats. Nation building exercise in India is essentially an attempt to strengthen national integration, the political aspect of which has been accomplished but the socio-cultural and economic components of which continue to generate, unfinished struggles within the polity. The enormity of this challenge gives misgivings about the continuation of political integration of the Indian nation state. In fact, the 'Cultural sub-nationalism' of the sub-continent, even after partition, continues to threaten 'Political Nationalism' and its viability to survive as a nation-state. The political nation-state of India has to struggle with cultural sub-nation groups of its plural society and buy time so that economic nationalism may sprout and cultural sub-nationalism of the sub-continent may give way to create larger politico-economic entities of viable nature.[8]

One of the major source of generating anti-democratic forces in the form of terrorism threatening the stability, integrity and security of our country is 'Majority revivalism' and 'minority fundamentalism'.

The problem of Indian minorities has three levels of awareness (i) the grievance situation, (ii) the identity crisis, (iii) homeland dream through secession. However, it is the last one which succumbing to militant means becomes a threat not only to governabilty but to the very existence of a nation. The terrorism in Punjab with its massive killings and destruction entailing huge cost for the country in terms of human, organisational and financial resources has to be linked to such perspective.

Though generically, the Khalistan oriented terrorist movement in Punjab is not much different from other socio-political group conflicts and other terrorist movements that India has faced so far in its modernisation and political development. That is the difference on account of its theocratic content.[9] Complicated by the realities of the Indian history, both pre and post independence, the nature of economic development in that state, the nature of evolution of politics and political development in it, the advancement of the Sikh migrants abroad, Pakistan's retaliative posture with reference to its contiguity to the state and the remotely and latently encouraging environment of certain circles of high international politics.

One of the major factors responsible for the Sikh militancy is our definition of secularism which believes not in separation of politics and religion but assigns an active role to religion in political field. Consequently, religion has been used and misused for political gains. Secularism in India went on developing a clear slant or what may be viewed as appeasement of communalism (parochial loyalities of the various religious groups to their religions rather than to the polity).

The historical background of the Akali movement in Punjab in the course of India's nationalist movement was appreciated and encouraged by the mainstream.[10] This is the first historical base of legitimacy of what is being flaunted today as the issue of Sikh identity. The second legitimacy of the national movement successfully dissuated Sikhs from making any serious move for Sikhistan[11] or Khalistan. The third basis of legitimacy has been the grievance of Sikh community that a Punjabi suba was not created after the reorganisation of states on the linguistic basis for long and, in the meantime, the leaders who agitated to demand for such a statehood were humiliated.[12] The fourth basis has been that the inter-group conflict — the non Sikh Punjabis getting Hindi recorded as their mother tongue in the census thereby hurtening the sentiment of the co-linguist Sikhs.[13] The issues of Chandigarh, share in river water for irrigation and industrial non-investment in agriculturally productive and affluent Punjab[14] etc., have also added to the rising legitimacy of the Sikh cause based on militancy promoted by historical and religious traditions of marital spirit, heroic struggles against tyranny and religious catering for martyrdom. The frustration of the Akalis following the return of the Congress(I) to power[15], the shabbiness of internal rivalries of the Congress(I) intermeshing its leadership, at points, with the fundamentalists[16] and the external environment, gave a great fillip to the legacy of the Sikh demand for greater autonomy formulated in more and more crystalized fashion with the advancement of the 1970s and the advent of 1980s. Such was the soil on which the terrorist movement for Khalistan grew.

As in the case of all terrorist movements, a key element in the strategy of Khalistan terrorism was to create terror, to undermine the authority of the administration and to demonstrate their own strength. The strategy of Khalistani terrorists, however, contained other key element also specific to them. One is to appear as defender of Sikhs and Sikh religion, to widen the gulf between Hindus and Sikhs, to create a situation in which large scale Hindu-Sikh riots break out, to force Hindus of Punjab to migrate to other states and to create a situation in which Sikhs from other states are also forced to migrate and encouraged to do so.

They started by killing Nirankaris including Nirankari Sikhs because orthodox Sikhs have strong prejudice against them. Then it was the turn of Hindus in general and such individual personalities whose killings would provoke Hindus in and outside Punjab into senseless violent acts against innocent Sikhs.

Though the state is back to normalcy but the state of affairs as existed till late 1980s put a question mark on the claims of India as a successful democracy, its secular polity, efficiency of administrative, intelligence and governing bodies as well as the loyalty to the democratic values/ norms, to the respective state system and patriotism of the minority communities (religious/ethnic). The various issues related with Punjab terrorism have been studied (causes, governmental strategy) in juxtaposition with the issue of political development or decay, during the period of militancy there. The point is to analyse the manner in which 'Religion' is used as a tool for political expediency and how the grievances of minorities are given communal overtones by the political elites to grab and sustain their control over power. How religious fundamentalism leads to 'legitimacy' and 'structural crisis' resulting in the erosion of effectiveness of administrative machinery in handling the demand load on the polity. Thus, loss of faith in the present state-system as well as loss of people's cooperation to the state administration, making it more vulnerable to disintegrating and anti-democratic forces. Though the terrorism in Punjab seems to have died down but the fact is that it is continuing in one way or the other putting a question mark on the governability and administrativeness of Indian state system.

References

1. P.N. Kathpalia, 'Counter Measures Against Terrorism', *Indian Defence Review*, Vol. II, 2, July 1987, p. 66.
2. Brian Jenkins, 'International Terrorism, Trend and Potentialities', Santamonica, California, *Rand Corp. 1977*, p. 38.
3. *Ibid.*, p. 43.
4. *Ibid.*
5. Paul Wilkinson, 'Terrorism: International Dimension' in William Gulteridge, (Ed.), *The New Terrorism*, Monsel Publication, Ltd., London 1986, p. 33.
6. Nath, Shaileshwar, *Terrorism in India*, National Publishing House, Delhi, 1980.
7. S.C. Tiwari, *Terrorism in India*, South Asian Publications, New Delhi, 1990.
8. Moin Shakir, *Politics of Minorities*, Ajanta Publication, Delhi, 1980.
9. K.L. Taneja, *Sikh Politics* (1920-1940), Vishal Publication, Kurukshetra, 1984, p. 124; Sachchidanand Sinha et al. *Army Action in Punjab : Prelude and Aftermath*, Samta Era Publication, New Delhi, 1984, pp. 14-15.
10. K.L. Taneja, n. 9, pp. 173-96.
11. Sachchidanand Sinha et al. n. 9, pp. 16-17; Shalender Singh, *Khalistan : An Academic Analysis*, Amar Prakashan, New Delhi, 1982, pp. 35-39.
12. Sachchidanand Sinha et al., n. 9, p. 31.
13. Shalender Singh, n. 11, pp. 93-105.
14. *Ibid.*, pp. 85-92.
15. *Ibid.*
16. D.P. Sharma, *The Punjab Story*, APH Publication, New Delhi, 1996.

2

Genesis of the Problem

The word 'Sikhs' derived from the Prakrit -Sikkha which in Sanskrit became Sishya meaning disciple. It grew as a new sect around 'Hinduism' but outside it. The religion was evolved by a sucession of ten gurus. The credit, infact, goes to Guru Nanak for the creation of this sect/religion. However, the contribution of sixth Guru is worth mentioning here as he was the one who combined temporal and spiritual authorities by putting two swords — one on the right and the other on the left — combining Meeri and Peeri (temporal, and spiritual authorities). From this time onwards Sikhs continued to combine religion and politics. Likewise the seeds of separate identity were sown by Guru Gobind Singh. He inspired his folk men with faith and gave them five Ks as a distinct mark — Kes (long hair), Kangha (comb), kripan (sword), kachcha (short dramers) and kara (steel bracelets) and thus created Khalsa on April 13, 1699 at Anandpur Sahib. He baptised the five devotees and got himself baptised from them by giving power to the 'sangat to over-rule the Guru and thus created real democracy. This is how one can trace the course of politicisation of religion or the fusion of religion and politics in Sikhism as well as the development of militant attitude amongst Sikhs.[1]

MISL or territorial confideracies which were created during 1745-1767, a period which saw about 9 Afghan invasions, determine to the large extent the Sikh socio-political expectations even today. MISL were created to defend the Sikh territory from any kind of invasion. In times of strife local leaders organised the bands of able bodied Sikhs, initially to fight against Afghans or Mughals and ultimately to fight with each other. However, the idea of MISL became firmly embodied in the minds of Sikhs as accepted, recognisable way of organising for conflicts. The present day factionalism in Punjab politics is the modern equivalent to these ancient confideracies. A knowledge of 18th century MISL sets pattern for and legitimises the modern factionalism in politics. 'We are behaving, people may say to themselves' as our fore-bears did when one MISL struggled against another in former glorious times'.[2]

While the above mentioned facts reflect the development of violent methods and struggles for safeguarding their life, liberty and property as well as fusion of religion and politics, there were other factors responsible for the development of 'threat to the religious identities', largely associated with the issue of the control and management of Gurudwaras.

Gurudwaras acquired great significance after Guru Gobind Singh's procalamation of Granth Sahib as the eternal Guru and became the pivot of Sikh social life as this was the place where sacred book was housed. Many gurudwaras were run by Hindu Mahantas (supervisors) or those who had abandoned their outward symbols of five Ks and became indistinguishable from Hindus. The properties of the gurudwaras came to be recorded in their names.

Perception of a grave threat to their religious identities because of the above mentioned reason paved way for the setting up of Shiromani Gurudwara Prabandhak Committee (SGPC) to manage the Golden Temple in 1920. Few months later 'Akali Dal' or the army of the faithful or immortal was created to wrest control of gurudwaras from the Mahants.[3]

Simultaneously the campaign run by some Hindu communal forces to deny the emergence of Sikhism as an independent religion let to a growing fear amongst the Sikh elites that the sikhs might be absorbed in the Hindu social system.

This is how, historically speaking, sikhs started perceiving themselves as separate people. The Sikhs have been trying to obtain recognition of this distinct identity for decades. The underlying objective of the struggle thus was political power.

There were various other factors which provided fuel to the otherwise dormant demand for independent recognition of Sikh identity in the post-independence era which by the decade of late 1970s took the form of 'Khalistan'. The causes behind can be analysed under following categories.

I) Imperial Conspiracy

British imperialist who ruled India till 1947 did all they could to keep Indian people divided and to weaken their unity in the fight for independence. As a part of this policy of 'divide and rule', the British ruler and their spokesmen made persistent efforts to plant communal feelings in the minds of the people.

The rivalry between Hindu leaders or Mahantas and Sikhs, whereby growth of Sikhism as an independent religion was denied, was fully utilised by British to inculcate, encourage and strengthen the false and reactionary concept of an independent political identity of the Sikhs.

Against this background added with the demand of Pakistan by Muslim League, Akalis too demanded 'Azad Punjab' in 1942 when Cripps Mission arrived in India. The Sikhs were encouraged by the British to regard themselves as a totally distinct and separate nation. They made persistent efforts to inculcate among the people the dangerous idea of religion as the basis of nation-states.

Militancy And Religion

The perception of Sikhs with regard to their political world and motivation is deep rooted in their cultural and religious traditions in which militant politics has been regarded as an inseparable part of politics ever since the days of Guru Govind Singh. Another related factor is the importance of the 'Khalsa Identity'. According to Sudhir Kakkar the 'Two elements militancy and martyrdom are its inner counterparts of the well known five Ks which constitute the outer marks of the Khalsa Identity.[4] Since the days of the great Guru Govind Singh, one dying for the cause of the panth is glorified and treated as a martyr. On this ground terrorists in Punjab justified their inhuman acts of violence and genocide. This is how they tried to acquire mass recognition to the element of 'Independent Punjab'.

Militancy and religion, as a matter of fact have always been a part of Akali politics in Punjab during the post-independence period. Sikhs always resorted to militant posture in order to achieve their goals whatever they may be, what is new is not militancy rather its increased dimension, intensity, changed objectives. It also carries the explanation of extremist and terrorist facing little difficulty in adopting militancy and the rationale behind their appeal to the psyche of the Sikh masses in highly subjective terms in the name of religious prestige and honour of the panth.[5]

The relationship between religion and militancy or religion and politics thus paved for a significant role to be played by 'Akal Takht'. The Takht is regarded as the seat of both spiritual and secular powers. Besides, Akal Takht is also the seat of theocratic education in Punjab where the children of small, rural peasants get the education completely based on Sikh scriptures and rituals, devoid of modern education and scientific outlook. Granthis, ragis and priests appointed at various gurudwaras, are also the product of this institution, who are important players in the politico-religious affairs of Punjab.[6]

This tradition continued in post-independence period with consitutional backing for such provisions. Article 30 of our constitution safeguards the right of minorities to establish and administer their educational institutions.[7]

These traditions made the task of Sikh terrorists much easier since they had a very legitimate channel (Akal-Takht) to get their ideas accepted and recognised at the grass root level; they were able to influence the common man once religious elite was under their control. Religious confirmity to militancy in Punjab helped it both in its initiation and sustainance.

Religious Fundamentalism

Fundamentalism was what made the situation explosive in Punjab. The fundamentalist religious revivalism is a universal phenomenon. All great world religions are going through a revivalist phase. Islam, Hinduism, Christianity and even the Sinhalese Buddhists have felt its stirrings. In Punjab the rise of sant Bhindaranwale was a phenomenon that has a lot in common with the Iranian model. Modernity brings in its wake a certain amount of westernization, capitalism, and a consumer based society not concerned with have nots. A fringe society of jean-clad and smack taking youth emerges, who have no rapport with the old order. The Iranian Revolution was what religious fundamentalist felt was the 'Maghrib Zhadgi' or over westernization of the Shah of Iran. The Bhindaranwale movement also, was based upon a return to the old Puritanical values. The second common feature, was the use of religious places and organisations as a base for political and extremist activity. It created the atmosphere of intolerence threatening the secular fabric of our society and governability[8].

Socio-Economic Factors

Partition deprived many of the Sikhs of their land and homes. Hard work and initiative restored their prosperity. Green Revolution strategy has been highly successful in Punjab. Rich peasantary led to the growth of regional leadership as well as demand for industrial development which was completely neglected in Punjab. After agricultural production reached its optimum, demand for big industries and for 'agro-industries' grew at large. Akali leaders started saying that, 'when we produce agricultural goods why should we have not the rights to sell them at the highest available price in the international market ? Why should we be forced to sell our produce to the Government of India at the price fixed by it for deficit Indian states ?' Clearly this is a demand for profiteering prices as distinct from the very justified demand of the peasantary for remunerative prices.[9]

Similarly the landlords and the kulaks have been demanding greater share in the state power who were already a dominant force in the economy of the state and wanted to be as dominant in the power structure of the state. They want to rule the state and want Punjab under their hegemony. But this desire for greater power-share was not centred to regional level rather it took national overtones, some developed all India interest including industrial interest. Thus, power demand manifested itself in various shades from regional autonomy to secession or independent statehood.[10]

Along with economic prosperity there has been a marked increase in the levels of literacy in Punjab as elsewhere in the country in the last few decades. This has led to a class of semi-educated rural youth who are not prepared to take up the traditional pursuits of agriculture. Yet white collar or blue collar jobs are not available in such numbers so as to absorb them all. There is thus a large reservoir of discontented, educated unemployed youth. This is a dangerous and volatile mass which is angry, turbulent and can be easily manipulated. This is the fishing ground for naxalites, religious fundamentalists and terrorists. The bulk of the terrorists in Punjab (particularly the youth wings) have come from this category. This mass of educated but unemployed youth is not just confined to Punjab.

Socio-economic factors led to the naxalite movement in West Bengal, Tilangana, Andhra Pradesh and in some other parts of India. North East is still under violence due to the prevailing socio-economic factors there. They contributed also the violent situation in Punjab.[11] Despite tremendous sucess of Green Revolution in Punjab such kind of socio-economic tensions are a paradox that need a separate and independent analysis.

Class Character Of The Problem

The case of Punjab is not like Bihar where we are witnessing an upsurge of the landless against the rich farmers. Had it been so we would have seen a line-up of the poorer Mazabhi and Ramdassi Sikhs against the richer Jat and Khatri classes. The bulk of the terrorists recruits have come from the more prosperous Jat and Khatri Sikh classes. Over the years the Akali party has come to represent Jat and Khatri Sikh interest[12]. Success of Green Revolution was largely the result of their hard work. And yet the Green Revolution is petering out because of two factor :

(a) Fragmentation Of Land Holdings :

Punjab's 70% of agricultural land is owned by a small number of people while the rest of the land by majority of poor farmers and share croppers. The average size of the land holding of the poor farmers is 5 acres farm. With the pressure of increasing population and social moves these are getting further broken up. Below 5 acres farm is not economically viable. Hence, out of the two to three sons that a farmer may have the farm can support just one. With just one son on farm, the others must find employment elsewhere. That employment is not forthcoming. Hence the dissatisfaction that finally leads to despair and extremism.[13]

(b) Rural Indebtedness :

The Green Revolution in Punjab has been financed by bank loans. Bank loans enabled the farmers to buy tractors, threshers, fertilisers, pesticides, seeds and other inputs required. Rural peasantry was thus under a heavy debt burden. Repayment of debt and the interest became a problem as the price of produce fails to keep pace with the price of inputs. An acre under the rice/wheat cycle yields at best Rs.7000 per annum. To that extent disturbed conditions suited the rich peasantry not only in Punjab but elsewhere in the country as well. They forced the government to ensure constant supply of agricultural inputs as well as to maintain a minimum support price. If pushed far enough they could force the Government to even cancel their loans. The rural rich were under a heavy burden. The farmer with small holdings were equally affected, in fact, more so. Their collective anxiety is at the root of a lot of Punjab's unrest. What is required was/is a quick solution on the part of government to force the pace of land-reforms or to re-shape it, so that share of land can be given to the landless.[14]

Economic grievances were given commercial overtones. A big majority of the Punjab peasants and landlords is Sikhs. Politically, a small section of it has been with the Congress, majority with the Akali Dal and even the Akali Dal leadership in the hands of rural rich, the Kulakas and the landlords. A big majority of the peasantary is also Sikh by religion and Jats by caste. While most of the agricultural labourers belong to the scheduled caste. Thus, caste and religion, economic crisis, proved to be important tools in the hands of Akalis who were able to rally behind them, the middle and the poor peasants and other Sikhs as well. Even non-religious demands were presented as the demands of the Sikhs. They tried to justify their agitation for more power and freedom on the ground that :

1. Centre discriminates against Punjab because Punjab's majority is that of the Sikhs, and their demands are not accepted because Sikhs are treated as second class citizens. On the economic front anti-people economic policies of the government leading to growing disparities, unemployment, atrocities on weaker section, corruption and too much of bureaucratisation led to grave discontentment especially amongst rural youth;

2. For Sikhs, religion and politics are inseparable.

   Therefore, economic crisis and other grievances, despite sepectacular success of 'Green Revolution', were given religious colours. Not only government but also the Hindu residents of Punjab were held responsible for their misery. Gradually they came over the conclusion that a greater share in power-structure of the nation can be helpful in resolving their problems. This feeling was infact ignited and given fuel by the political elites of Punjab who had vested interest. Thus, worsening economic state of majority was utilised by top political strata for political expediency by giving it religious and political colours. Soon they started propogating the thesis-'Sikhs—a separate nation' and 'the Sikh must have separate political identity' (not only religious identity) and demand 'Khalistan'. The origin of this theory is rooted in the history of Punjab since Britishers conquered Punjab from a Sikh ruler and the Sikh must rule Punjab again.[15]

Political Factors

An analysis of political factors shows that what has happened in Punjab is a failure of our attempts to secularise politics in the country. We have failed to break the nexus between religion, caste and politics. The legacy of the British strategy of 'divide and rule' affects our politics even today. Though the seeds of religious separartism as a basis for political demands were sown by the British, who did their best to preserve the Sikhs as an exotic in Indian milieu. Most of the political parties use religion, caste and such parochial values for the purpose of political expediency in the post-independence era. The most depressing features has been the collusion between some unscrupulous politicism (e.g. Akalis in Punjab) and the criminal elements of society, the smugglers, racketeers and illicit brewers. Flow of illegal money and muscle power in Indian politics, and the criminilisation of politics is the distinguishing feature of our political fabric today. In Punjab the bulk of such people joined the separatist movement to furnish their cause of smuggling and trafficking. The charismatic hold of sant Bhindaranwale over the Sikh masses was well exploited and made him some sort of a patron backed by number of Sikhs in foreign countries especially United States of America (USA), Canada, and United Kingdom (UK). The Congress party of India used this movement to frighten the Hindus to vote for them.

After the creation of the Punjabi Suba the Akali party came to power thrice in the state but had always to be supported by the Congress and once the BJP. None of these governments were permitted to last its normal tenure. This was also to be the fate of the only election won by Akalis with the required majority in 1985 where it was able to form its own government without the support of any other party. But the subsequent events led to the fall of Barnala Ministry with which stress on the Akalis increased internally and party was split into various factions.

Meanwhile, Bhindaranwale, who proved to be a Congress frankestein later on assumed leadership of the extremist. He was encouraged by the Congress for two reasons :

1. It would finish the moderate leadership of the Akalis,
2. It would embarrass Darbara Singh, the political rival of Zail Singh.[16]

The strategy of Congress party to rule the Punjab was based on the following tactics :

1. It enjoyed a fairly good percentage of Hindu votes, practically all scheduled caste votes including a minority of Sikh votes. Hence, their policies were tilted in favour of above mentioned category;

2. To impress the Sikh voters that it always gave Chief Ministership to a Sikh
3. It supported Sikh fundamentalism trying to prove that Congress Sikhs were more true to their faith than the Akali Sikhs. No Akali Chief Minister in the Punjab pondered so much to Sikh fundamentalism as the Congress Chief Minister Zail Singh. In 1980 elections Bhindaranwale compaigned for the Congress and even government funds and resources were used to promote him;
4. Posts of honour were always given to the Sikhs to appease them but attention to their genuine socio-economic requirements was more or less completely lacking;
5. A small microscopic minority even raised the demand for Khalistan.

The year of 1977 was a watershed year in the politics of Punjab giving rise to extremism when Bhindaranwale was given a political push by the Congress. He inherited the organisation of 'Damdami Taksal'[17] which was increasingly militant in nature. Bhindaranwale and Khalistan group were separate identities and it was much later that the two converged into one. Because of his religious differences with Nirankaris there developed a rift between Bhindaranwale and the Akalis which was filled by Congress.

Trained in a fundamentalist tradition, head of a theocratic institution—Akal Takht—which is also the pivot of Punjab politics, Bhindaranwale got an audience among the rural Sikhs and started pursuing fundamentalist policies. A sizeable number of youths were recruited who had no other outlets for creating utilization of their abundant energy. The vote politics of Punjab led to competing communalism by the Akalis and the Congress. In March 1981 Shiromani Gurudwara Prabandhak Committee (SGPC) declared Sikh as a separate nation and complained of discrimination against Sikh.[18] By 1982 Sant Bhindaranwale openly started using such choicest Akali agitational words as were used by the other Akali leaders such a 'tyranny', 'slavery', 'holy war' etc. to influence the Sikh psyche. These words had already become the idioms of Punjab politics.

Role Of Akali Dal

The first political party exclusively representing the Sikh community was formed (Akali Dal) in early twenties which provided a platform for the assertion of a separate Sikh identity, but at the same time created a minority complex among the Sikh community. Sikh fear of losing this identity in a pre-dominantly Hindu India became sharpened when political power continued to erode the Akali Party even in Punjab. This turned the Akali energies into organising political agitations at regular interval on various issues—political, economic agrarian, linguistic and religious in order to broaden their areas of influence. All such agitations had only one single objective to promote the legitimacy of the Sikh desire to rule in Punjab and were rooted in a supposed denial of the perceived claims to political supremacy in the state.

Before independence the Akali party functioned as adjunct of the Indian National Congress. After independence and partition in 1947, there were rumblings of discontent in the Akali party due to wooing of Akalis by the Congress party, the major segment of which stayed away from the Congress. The gulf between Congress and the Akali party continued to grow till it became nearly unbridgeable in the 1970s. Mrs. Indira Gandhi used two well thought out strategies to finish off the Akalis as a viable Sikh political party which could challenge designs of the Congress party to rule the Punjab.

1. She encouraged the growth and expansion of the Sikh extremist movement by giving covert support to Bhindaranwale and;
2. When he became uncontrollable, took to large scale killings and plunder and established a reign of terror in the Punjab, she ordered Army to flush out the terrorists from the holiest Shrine of the Sikhs, the Golden Temple.

She largely succeeded in her designs. The Akali party which representated the moderate segment of Sikhs became irrelevant in Punjab. Inevitably the extremists gained ground as the Akali party became non-functional for quite some time. The army action in this background made Sikh community in India and abroad discontented, sullen, angry and alienated.

Extremism, thus, had an open field to spread out its roots aggressively. Harvinder Ahuja observes that 'The Akalis and the extremist were at the root cause of the entire crisis, the Akalis for daily raising, reiterating and renewing their demands without realising their significance and repercussions. Everyone knows, they never raised any demand when they were ruling in Punjab but once out of power, they suddenly became votaries of the Sikh cause. One of the biggest crimes is to have blurred the distinction between the Sikh religion and politics. The Akali Dal is and always was a political party and whatever the Akalis were asking for was all political in nature and based on a desire for power in Punjab. They shamelessly gave a religious facade to it and mouthed their demands from inside the holy places. They exploited the peasantary and the illiterate Sikh masses by raising the bogey of the panth in danger. Whenever they issued a call for agitation, it was always addressed to the Sikhs and not to their own party men'.[19] The role of Akali Dal in Punjab politics to turn to violence was so great that it needs a separate analysis.

Decay Of Morality

The growth of extremism in youth in India since 1947 is co-terminous with the decay of morals in India. An unjust system reeking with corruption is enough to produce terrorists against their own government. In the presence of unprincipled and rapacious politicians and bureaucrats who enjoyed both power and influence, the disgust of idealistic youth was natural. Increasing role of money and muscle power caused much frustration amongst the youth. The link between rampant corruption and youth extremism is clear. Extremism in Punjab was linked to a extent to the attitudinal changes, moral decaying in the youths who were targeted by the leaders of Khalistani movement for the recruitment for terrorism.

Role of Ex-Servicemen

This is the single most important and vital factor. It is one of the most significant factor as each year approximately 60,000 servicemen are released from service. A fair proportion of these go to the Punjab. Due to the imperatives of keeping a young profile in the service, servicemen are retired relatively early. Since the military is a closed micro society there are considerable readjustment problems faced by ex-servicemen, the biggest of which are the economic imperatives of settling down in a new civil environment. It can often lead to anxiety bordering on depression or neurosis and consequent adjustment problems. If the mass of the educated unemployed youth present a very lucrative fishing ground for fomenting trouble, the destabilisation potential of this trained military manpower is even more dangerous and how dangerous it has been was highlighted in Punjab. Two retired Major Generals of the Indian Army, Jaswant Singh Bhullar and Shabeg Singh, masterminded most of the terrorists' operations in the Bhindaranwale phase. Valuable military expertise, especially experience in insurgency type operations was available to them particularly in the person of Maj. Gen. Shabeg Singh, who had gained vast experience in low-intensity operations in Nagaland and in the 1971 India-Pakistan War. It was this that lent such a dangerous aspects to the unrest in Punjab. Serious attempts were made through religious fundamentalist and communal overtones to subvert the loyalties of serving and retired Sikh soldiers. The number of arms indigenously acquired by the terrorists were staggering and could not have been acquired without the ex-serviceman connection. Operation Metal became a full-scale conventional assualt which caused considerable casualties to our forces. No amount of smugglers and criminals could have generated such effective firepower and resistance. Interrogation reports of Pakistani trained terrorirsts indicate that Pakistani intelligence personnel were primarily looking for Sikh ex-servicemen. They have intelligence value and are being preferred for training and formation of hardcore terrorist cells. The phenomenon is not confined to Punjab alone. The recent rise of Subhas Ghising's Gorkha National Liberation Front is a grim warning of the dangerous potential of unemployed and disgruntled ex-servicemen who are recruited for anti-national/secessionist causes. There is an imperative need therefore to look after our ex-servicemen and continue their 'education' in the realms of national integration, patriotism, democratic and secular values and respect for other religions. Much is being done for rehabilitation of ex-servicemen, but far more needs to be done to assuage the bitterness of being unwanted and forgotten. This breeds alienation and alienation among trained military manpower can be exploited by the dis-integrative forces. The Government and the Army need to reach out to our ex-servicemen, to identify their problems and take meaningful steps to resolve them.

1980-84, Period of Sikh Alienation

This was the period when many incidents took place which alienated Sikh masses and were made to perceive in those incidents a real threat to their identity—humiliation of Sikh soldiers during Asiads in Haryana, opposition of Hindu organisations on the ban of smoking in and around Golden Temple complex, the breaking of Golden Temple Replica at Chandigarh railway station, burning the picture of Guru Ramdas. In this background Bhindaranwale said, 'Sikhs were second class citizens and slaves in India and that they must fight for their independence. Our aim is to break the shackles of this slavery'.[20]

Thus Bhindaranwale's fight against the Central Government was not too far removed from Sikh struggle which since the 10th Guru has been mostly viewed in the images of 'lifting up the sword' against the tyrannical rules. The sense of grievances and alienation increased manifold after the Operation Blue Star in 1984 which completely shook the sikh psyche. To quote Khushwant Singh, 'now it will be increasingly difficult to find a self-respecting Sikh who will have a kind word to say for the government. Sikhs will feel isolated and a separate people'.[21] This army action was exploited by the leaders of independence to the maximum advantage for their cause, alienating the Sikhs from the mainstream, justifying their demand for Khalistan.

Unjust Re-Organisation

The re-organisation of Punjab in November 1966 was not appreciated by the Sikhs. Chandigarh was made a union territory. Many Punjabi speaking villages/areas were given to Haryana while many Hindi speaking villages came to Punjab largely because Tehsil not village was made the basis of division and secondly large number of Hindus had got recorded Hindi as their mother tongue.

While Akali Dal leader Master Tara Singh came out with a demand for a Sikh-Suba which was later on modified to a Punjabi speaking province in which Sikh should be atleast 60% of the population and Punjabi language — the mother tongue of all Punjabis (Sikhs + Hindus). Hindu communalists on the other hand, made the false assertion that Hindi and not Punjabi was their mother tongue. They too gave religious colour to the entire issue. Many (Hindu) Congress leaders refused to consider Punjabi as their official language, even with the option to use the Devnagri script. Against the demand for a Sikh majority 'Punjabi Suba', a demand for 'Maha-Punjab' in which Sikhs would be microscopic minority was advanced.

Thus, in this manner, the issues of language and of formation of Punjabi-speaking state were highly politicised to assume heavy communal overtones. Punjabis got communally divided. Consequently re-organisation of state on linguistic basis was much delayed though it was an old promise of the Congress. Not only was it delayed but led to widespread differences between the two communities—Hindu Punjabis and the Sikh Punjabis.

There is no doubt that Punjab had certain genuine grievances e.g. (1) Chandigarh, (2) distribution of river water, (3) Proper demarcation of Punjabi speaking areas and (4) a few religious demands. The Congress government was willing to give a favourable verdict on most of these problems but they wanted to make it a quidpro-quo for an electoral deal. While the Akalis combined religion with politics, the government of India was equally guilty of getting advantages for the Congress party out of the performance of its duties as the Government. The negotiation between the two dragged on and the Akalis used this to impress upon their followers that they could get no justice from the Hindu dominated Government.

The vote politics of Punjab, thus, led to competing communalism by the Akalis and the Congress. The Congress was unable to deal with the problem firmly and objectively as it always hoped to strike an electoral deal with them.[22]

Punjab underwent a decade of extremism and violence due to various politico-religious and other related factors. Infact, it has no single or common cause. Its causes were diverse, often one cause overlaping another or several causes.

References

1. D.P. Sharma, *The Punjab Story Today*, APH Publication, New Delhi 1996, pp. 3-7.
2. *Ibid.*, pp. 5-6.
3. Satyapal Deng, *Genesis of Terrorism in Punab*, Patriot Publication, New Delhi 1988, p.2.
4. Rajani, R. Jha, 'Origin and Dimension of Terrorism, The Punjab Case' in S.C. Tiwari, *Terrorism in India*, South Asian Publication, New Delhi, 1990, p.116.
5. *Ibid.*, p.135.
6. Gopal Singh, 'Terrorism in Punjab : Supposed Modus Operendi and Objectives', *Mainstream*, 24 July, 1988.
7. S.C. Tiwari, n. 4, pp. 134-36.
8. Madan Gaur, *Pointers in Punjab*, Press and P.R. Service Publication, 1985, pp. 4-9.
9. Verinder Grover, *The Story of Punjab : Yesterday and Today*, vol. II, Deep and Deep Publication, New Delhi,1995, pp. 24-25.
10. Satya Pal Deng, n. 3, pp. 117-18.
11. S.C. Tiwari, n.4, p. 128.
12. Verinder Grover, n.9, pp. 36-37.
13. IDR Research Team- Punjab : Profile of Terrorist Movement', *Indian Defence Review*, vol. II, July 1987.
14. *Ibid.*
15. Verinder Grover, n. 9, pp. 71-80.
16. D.P. Sharma, n. 1, p. 26-27.
17. 'Damdami Taksal Sect' preaches strict adherence to Sikh tenets. Sect which has the militant, religious, political ideology and the sanction of violence for its persual gradually led to the emergence of Sant Bhindaranwale cult in Punjab as promoter of terrorism. Its members are fanatic, hard core believers in violence.
18. N.S. Saksena, *Terrorism History and Facets*, Abhinav Publication, New Delhi, 1985, pp. 179-81.

19. Harvinder Ahuja, ' Reflections on Punjab', *Indian Express*, New Delhi, July 23, 1984.
20. N.S. Saksena, n. 18, pp. 189-198; S.S. Uban, 'A matter of Honour', *Hindustan Times*, New Delhi,18 January, 1987.
21. Khushwant Singh, 'Tears Win a pool of Nector', *Indian Express*, New Delhi,17 June, 1984.
22. N.S. Saksena, 'Dangerous illustrations About Terrorism', *Times of India*, New Delhi, April 10,1984.

3

Government Strategy

Dealing with terrorism is not any easy task because terrorism is not the result of just one factor. It is rather the product of a combination of factors. As such a multipronged strategy to deal with the problem at psychological, social, political, economic and security level is required. Experiences of Punjab, North East and other places like Northern Ireland, Sri Lanka, Lebanon, Algeria etc. are indicative of the fact that regarding terrorism only as a security problem is not going to solve it. Dealing with it from purely military point of view is no answer to it. This approach alienates the people because repressive powers may also be rightly or wrongly, used against innocent people thereby forcing the alienated people to join hands with terrorists. It also creates sympathy for them. Besides this, the repressive measures undertaken by the government are condemned by human rights activists and other organisations. Unfortunately for most of time our government relied more on military solution to Punjab problem.

Operation Blue Star[1]

When the problem in Punjab started hotting up in the early 1980s, unanimous view was that army involvement would not be in the interest of the organisation or the territory and that should it be involved it would lead to trouble in some units.

It is a historic fact now that the army was asked to get itself involved, setting unprecedented standards in the scale and scope of its involvement. The state-wide curfews of long duration, the massive scale of deployment of armed forces, the use of excessive force in Operation Blue Star, and the virtual handing over of the civil administration to the army was unprecedented army activity to deal with an internal problem. It is inconceivable that a democratic government could adopt such measures. But this was merely the setting for the even harsher measures adopted thereafter which have had a very questionable effect on the Punjab situation.

If the repercussions and adverse fall out were taken lightly, the political and military leadership is to be held quilty of not being in touch with reality, a most dangerous shortcoming in any leadership.

The use of armed forces has been made several times for the defence of the country but neither the government of India nor our army have had to face the type of situation that they had to deal within Punjab. This time action had to be taken against our own people. Perhaps, the realization of this fact was responsible for its delay and a cause of hesitation for taking such step. But then there was no way out. By about the middle of 1983 anti-national and terrorist groups, which had come into being as a consequence of the growth of fundamentalism and separatism had established control over the Golden Temple and converted it as the main base of their operations. It was said that 'If it continues at the present rate, the Sikh terrorism in Punjab will have cost more lives in two years than the IRA campaign in Northern Ireland has cost in twenty'.[2] Cult of violence and hatred spread rapidly and at a macro-level in Punjab. Akal Takht was occupied by Bhindaranwale and his followers who were practically out of bounds for the local police. Golden Temple provided a safe abode to them and their materials. With the fortification of the Golden Temple and a number of other gurudwaras, the systematic elimination of those who did not agree with their aims and methods and the raising of the cries of the 'Panth in Danger' it was evident that terrorists were aiming at something much more and bigger than merely getting some religious and territorial demands accepted.

Critics of Operation Blue Star forget that Golden Temple and other gurudwaras were used to offer immunity to terrorists and those who worked to disrupt the unity and integrity of the country. This has been an example without parallel of the misuse of religion and sacred places. This misuse of sacred places for anti-national activities opened up the issue to questions such as that 'whether it is right for places of worship to be used as store for arsenals or to transform them into sanctuaries for terrorists and anti-social elements.[3] Is it not the violation of the sanctity of constitution or the liberties granted by it? Whether armed action is necessary to meet out such challenges in view of the adverse effects it will have on those who owe allegience to their religion and places of worship. Views with regard to such questions were/are diverse, depending on the subjectivity of the person involved in debate.

Impact :

The action of the government was justified as well as unaviodable. It also succeeded in flushing out the extremist who had entrenched themselves in the Golden Temple and other gurudwaras and spread out all over Punjab and brought much needed relief to the inhabitants of the state who had been living in constant fear and panic.

Such use of religious places also put a question mark on the effectivity of our intelligence services. It was surprising that the government failed to trace out a true picture of happenings inside the Golden Temple. An imminent rebellion was under way for long term violence for separation.[4] It became unaviodable for the government not to resort to armed action.

The worst part of the Operation Blue Star was the severe damage caused to Darbar Sahib complex and the Akal Takht. It also had very worst effects on the Sikh psyche. The loss of the Sikh library with its rare and irreplaceable documents was particularly a damaging blow to Sikh history/heritage. All this left the Sikhs full of anger and resentment. The immediate reaction of Operation Blue Star was one of the dismay and anguish. The Sikhs not only in Punjab but everywhere were outraged and shocked. The most serious reaction was in the Army. Sikh soldiers in large number deserted the Army units and headed towards Amritsar. A serious crisis of discipline was created, apart from doubting the suitability of Sikh for military and other sensitive services.

It was a gross case of misuse of religious places for destroying the secular character of our polity which has granted enjoyment of freedom of religion to its every citizen. This also puts a question mark on the functioning of our democracy as a successful means for the preservation of the secularism in India as enshrined in our constitution.[5]

Those who condemn the army action or compare it with Jalianwala Bagh massacre paid no due consideration mainly to two things-

1. Golden Temple and other gurudwaras were being used to offer immunity to criminals, terrorists and those who worked to disrupt the unity and integrity of the country as well as of the piousness and sanctivity of the religion they claimed to be followers. In India's recent history it was this which necessitated the

government to take action against those terrorists hiding in the Golden Temple. Sanctity of the Golden Temple was not violated by the government but by those who were breaking the pride and dignity of the nation and their religion as well.

2. Jalianwala Bagh massacre involved the genocide of armless, innocent and patriotic people attending a peaceful assembly.

A realization later on grew that religious liberty and tolerance on the part of government and the masses in no way means the use of religious places by the people of any faith, to defy the authorities by turning them into armed fortresses. In fact, secularism will not survive in any country if a faith takes it on itself to destroy the essential unity and integrity of the country under any pretext. Misinterpretation of secularism and converting holy shrines into armed fortresses by a community like Sikh, who have disproportionately more men in armed forces, than they can legitimately said to be entitled to, may prove fatal to the security of nation. The action which the government has had to take in Punjab was neither against the Sikhs nor the Sikh religion, it was against terrorism and terrorists. Besides there was no alternative left with the government other than army action. The government infact in the beginning adopted a persuasive and counciliatary approach to the problem. Its failure led to the army action. Whatever its consequences it was a harrendous event in the history of independent India.

Operation Black Thunder

Operation Blue Star could not put an antidote to violence and genocide by the terrorists. The aggravating situation was once again made it necessary on the part of the government of India to undertake another armed action against the terrorists.

The election of G.S. Tohra to the presidentship of SGPC in 1986 injected new life into the secessionist movement in Punjab. Security forces were disbanded from regulating the entries of the Golden Temple complexs so that it could not be refused for anti-national activities. Tohra's election to SGPC was supported by terrorists. So he was under obligation to rehabilitate few of them into SGPC as its employees. This led to the occupation of complex of Golden Temple by terrorists. They started killing people inside the complex of the Temple. Torture and extortion started in big way.[6] Terrorism continued to grow, rather flared up unabated in the last of 1980s which witnessed the large scale killings of innocent people both Sikhs and Hindus. However this period was also marked significant due to three developments.

Firstly, the determination of the centre and the state to deal firmly with terrorists who were using the premises of the Golden Temple complex to further their secessionist activities as a consequence of which Operation Black Thunder was launched. Secondly, the introduction by the central government of legislation, in the form of ordinances such as the 'Religious Institutions (Prevention of Misuse) Ordinance and 'The Arms (Amendment) Ordinance 1988, which provide for capital punishment for causing death by use of illegal firearms and ammunition and enhances the maximum sentence for possession, use, sale and manufacture of prohibited arms ammunition to life imprisonment. And Thirdly, the state government's plan to clear a 300 mt. swathe around the Golden Temple complex of all buildings and construction, ostensibly to beautify the Temple surroundings but more so to ensure that in future the surrounding would not provide a hidden entry and exist into the complex, nor to be used by anti-national elements for armed struggle against the state.

As mentioned earlier the complex situation in Punjab drifted from bad to worse with no immediate prospects of solution in sight. Continuance of President's rule failed to improve the law and order situation in Punjab. The growth of violence was consistently on the ascent. Almost a pre-operation Blue Star situation emerged.

To meet out the situation Operation Black Thunder was launched in two series—First, in the wake of the declartion of Khalistan by the five member Panthic Committee from the precinct of the Golden Temple on April 29, 1986, and Second in May 1988. Task assigned to NSG (National Security Guard) was to flush out the undesirable elements from the premises of the Golden Temple complex. In addition to increasing pressure over the militants, the tactics adopted by the NSG was to search and destroy strong positions of the militants. They pinned down the militants to their rooms. At each stage precaution was taken to ensure that the sanctity of the holy shrine was not defiled and that loss of life was kept to minimum. Selective use of force was made. In all it was very planned and strategically executed operation.

The escalation in terrorist violence which became alarming in 1988 registered a definite reversal after Operation Black Thunder II. It exposed the hollowness of the militants regarding their commitment to their professed goal, their scant regard for the Sikh religion and traditions; and exploded the myth that they had created about themselves as being fearless, self-sacrificing crusaders of Sikh panth. Though the top militants disowned all those who surrendered during Operation Black Thunder II, it was no denying that the humiliating manner of surrender brought discredit to the militants in the eyes of the Sikh masses. A large number of terrorists listed out by the Punjab police were trapped in the Golden Temple complex at the time of Operation Black Thunder II.[7]

Though Operation Black Thunder too could not put an antidote either on the existing terrorist organizations or development of new ones. Fresh recruits were enlisted by the militant groups particularly by Khalistan Commando Force (KFC). But the most significant thing was the loss of centralised command of control. Most of the militant groups were plagued with mutual suspicion, accusations and rivalries. Dilution of the ideological content in the extremist activities also resulted in their degenerating into criminal and mercenary activities. Not only within the country but also outside polarisation was clearly visible in the militant organisations. Thus the year 1989 witnessed a progressive diminition in violent and militant activities of almost all the militant organisations.

But the trend of subdued extremist violence in the post 'Black Thunder-II' period proved to be a temporary phenomena. Last quarter of 1989 witnessed a steep increase in violence. Since October 1989 the declining graph of violence took a sharp upward curve and the situation was becoming more or less similar to that existed in pre-operation Black Thunder era. Terrorists activities were not only more aggressive but also more sophisticated in their techniques and factors. The kind of weapons they used were also highly sophisticated. There was a renewed supply of arms/ammunition/material and moral support from outside. Random and indiscriminate killing of security forces, officials, politicians and Hindus at large created terror and fear amongst Hindus living in Punjab. In this renewed phase of violence and terror, militants aimed at establishing parallel authority and administration (through levying taxes and revenues).

Despite such massive armed action like Operation Blue Star, Operation Wood Rose (in the rural areas to identify and round up suspected extremist, terrorists and their sympathisers) and Operation Black Thunder I and II government failed to put an antidote on militancy in the state. This is a reflection of the fact that in handling terrorist movements repression as a single point strategy had never succeeded susccessfully. Terrorist activities in the face of specific armed action underwent dormancy but resurfaced with great vigour afterwards.

Government always dealt the problem on an adhoc basis by employing and deploying more and more para-military forces/armed forces. A number of related factors like training, equipment and weaponary of these forces was not given due consideration. Only their strength was reviewed every time. Besides, government was primarily concerned with the curbing and combatment of violence, an outcome of various problems and factors. Problems responsible for terrorism were not properly attended and tackled. Though the political process which was initiated by the Government of India culminated into Rajiv-Longowal Agreement, 1986, collapsed due to the intensive opposition by the terrorist outfits and majority of the political leadership. This even led to the assassination of Sant Longowal. Later on the Government of India itself could not decidedly work for the implementation of the Agreement due to the opposition faced by it from Haryana. The assassination of Sant Longowal was a major event which rendered the political leadership ineffective, thereby paving the way for the terrorists to virtually have full control over the affairs of Punjab who were not ready to accept anything less than Khalistan.

Experiences show that at different times, rather in different situations, different measures were applied for dealing with the problem of terrorism. Some times, in some cases, purely military measures were applied. They achieved some success in some cases but in most they failed.[7] There are some practical problems involved with purely military measures to combat terrorism. Robert A. Fried Lander says that the state violence when directed against the individual endangers the like response.[8] It inevitably curbs the civil liberties which in turn generate or accentuate discontentment against the government, a highly desired objective of the terrorists who use the repressive measures of the government to propogandise that it is ruthless, cruel and does not care for us. Z.K. Zawodny points out that the more terror the government apply more figthers they produce.[9] This helps the sustenance of terrorism. This also remains one of the strategic objectives of the terrorists that if terrorism keeps going it may destabilise the economy and discredit the government. Moreover, pure military measures tend to create a feeling that the situation is getting out of hand.

A multipronged strategy is necessary for meeting out the threats of terrorism. It should be fought on different fronts—military, political, economic, social and psycological. If it has to be rooted out successfully a well coordinated efforts on all fronts should be undertaken by the government. And this relationship of coordination be maintained at every stage. This aspect was not given due and considerate consideration in case of Punjab by the government of India.

The first step towards this is to understand that no instant solution and miracles are possible. What is required is a proper perspective of the problem, proper organisation and utilization of the resources of the state to resolve the problem of terrorism. It also requires determination, patience, deep understanding of the issues and the people involved.

Understanding of the problem is as essential as the dealing with terrorism. It is very essential to analyse the political, social, economic, psychological, ideological and geographical factors which are involved in motivating the people to take up the arms. In other words the government must try to eliminate those grievances upon which the propogators of terrorism capatilise. Social and economic disparties often offer ready motivations to the population to participate in antinational activities.

Such problems which provide the cause of terrorism should be resolved. It is said that whatever the degree of dissatisfaction which forces the people to take up the arms against the government regime with the intention that through this means they can achieve what they are not getting otherwise, no leader of terrorism can offer to the people, the better politico-socio-economic conditions as the government can. The government should aim at severing the connections and linkages of the terrorists from the general public instituting such political, social and economic reforms which would establish governmental prestige and authority. This may result in alienating the population from the terrorist movement in developing public resistance against them. This might succeed in building up confidence in population about the government. The anti-national/disintegrative/separatist movements which India has faced since its independence to the large extent have been contained and tackled due to the effective action taken by the government to either rehablitate or divide, disorganise and broken the insurgents/terrorists groups through military, paramilitary and political offensives.

Terrorism aims at a target audience that is much wider than the available at the site of the terrorist violence. It aims at seeking maximum media coverage for their acts of violence to terrorise others and their cause for which they are committing violence. This is where the government must aim to strike, to minimise the consequences of the violence. Unnecessary and exagerated media coverage helps the terrorists in their fight against the regime. Media coverage for increasing the distribution of newspapers is an unprincipled activity against the interests of the nation. This should be given due consideration by the persons involved in media and by the government as well. A decade of terrorism in Punjab shows that role of media in dealing with it was not given proper consideration either by the government or the media itself.

Problem with terrorism is also that its theatre of operation is very large. It has globalised itself in its operations and support to it from external sources. It is needed to be tackled internationally. But unfortunately the response of international community to this problem has been more feeble and problematic. What to say about finding a solution to the problem, the community has quibbled over such questions as who is and is not a terrorist. Most states have remained unwilling to apply strict legal actions against terrorists. Not only this, many of the nations have a sympathetic attitude towards the political aspirations and objectives of groups who apply terrorism. This all has created obstacles for tackling terrorism. However the efforts have always been made to deal with it.

A general agreement for international cooperation is like a *sin qua non* for the effective prevention of international terrorism.[10] International legal response towards terrorism has largely been treaty based both bilateral and multilateral. Some international conventions like the Convention of

Offences and Certain Other Acts Committed on Boards Aircraft, Tokyo, September 14, 1963, the Convention for the Suppression of Unlawful Seizure of Aircraft, Hague, December 16, 1970, the Convention for the Suppression of Unlawful Acts against the Safety of Civil Aviation, Montreal, September 23, 1971, the Convention on the Prevention and Punishment of Crime. Against International Protected Persons including Diplomatic Agents, New York, December 1973, and International Convention against the Taking of Hostages, New York, December 17,1979 have no doubt promoted international cooperation which to some extent has contributed towards the combatment of terrorism internationally.

A general political will to uphold the rule of law to protect innocent and defeat the terrorism is very vital for the successful implementation of the treaties and conventions without which all treaties and conventions will not be worth the paper they are written on. International agreements against the specific terrorist actions are far more practical than attempt to outlaw terrorism as such. Punjab terrorism which was instigated from outside mainly by Pakistan and other NRI Sikhs generally based in England, United States of America and Canada was not tackled effectively at international level either due to the unwillingness, enmity between India-Pakistan and non-effective cooperation given by England and USA to the government of India. Concerted efforts of international level are also very essential for combating terrorism.

The other most important and effective means of prevention and tackling terrorism is the intelligence, which can provide a real time and actionable information. The intelligence-network should try to gain information prior to the onset of violence. If the intelligence is weak, the security forces can not act thus can only react as happened in Punjab with regard to the use of Golden Temple for violence by terrorists. Our intelligence network was not so effective in dealing with Punjab problem. Intelligence is a means to attack on the breading ground of terrorism. Its effective utilization is essentially necessary.

The Government of India dealt with the problem of terrorism in Punjab with its lack of determination and clear political vision in the beginning of the terrorism allowed it to continue in one form or the other. We can say the political ambitions of the then ruling party in Delhi were of prime consideration for it than the national interests. Though the terrorism to the most extent has been combated and tackled but it still continues to resurface in the form of sporadic terrorist violence.

References

1. A code name for the Army action into Punjab against terrorist based inside the Golden Temple. In Chakrata Commandos were trained on a large scale replication of the Golden Temple since April-May,1984.
2. Conor Cruise O 'Brien, 'Holy War Against India', Mainstream, September 1988, p.7.
3. Abida Saminuddin, *The Punjab Crisis, Challenges and Response,* Mittal Publications, New Delhi, 1985, p. 221.
4. N.S. Saksena, 'The Punjab Tragedy - I. Destroying the Police', Indian Express, New Delhi, July 19, 1984.
5. Madan Gaur, *Pointers in Punjab,* Press and P.R. Services Publication, 1984, pp. 132-136.
6. D.P. Sharma, *The Punjab Story,* APH Publication, New Delhi 1996, pp. 181-183.
7. Charles T.R. Bohannan, 'Anti-Gurrilla Operations', The Annals, vol. 341, May 1962, p. 23.
8. Robert A. Fried Landen, 'The Origin of International Terrorism' in Yonoh Alexander and Semmour Maxwell, *Terrorism : Interdisciplinary Perspective,* MacGraw-Hill Books Company Ltd., USA, p.31.
9. Z.K.Zawodny, 'Unconventional Warfare', in Henry A. Kissinger (Ed) *Problems of National Security,* Fredrick A. Praeger, USA, 1985, p. 341.
10. Akhtar Majeed, 'Tackling International Terrorism', Strategic Studies Journal, vol. 1, No.1, January, 1988, p. 98.

4

Militancy And Political Development In Punjab

The term governability in general refers to the integrative capacity of the political system to produce the desired result and to maintain the various contradiction (socio-economic, political) operating in the society. In other words, it refers to the enhanced capacity, especially of the administrative structure of the state to implement its policies and programme. In contrast to this definition the polity of developing countries over the years has witnessed the gradual erosion of its capacity to deliver the goods. Consequently, instead of political development these countries have undergone 'de-institutionalization'/ dis-intergration' of state structure. India is no exception and is facing 'structural crisis' and its related consequences of physical and cognitive violence in the form of communal riots, ethnic conflicts, group clashes, terrorism, insurgency and other socio-economic conflicts.

The dynamics of terrorism in Punjab can not be completely understood until perceived within this framework of political development/decay or 'structural crisis'. There exists a cause and effect relationship between the two. The overall political context had an impact on terrorism which in turn had rendered the democratic process in the state ineffective and meaningless during the period of terrorism there.

The Background

For much of the period of violence and terrorism, Punjab has not had a stable, elected government. The elected governments were either disintegrated or replaced by President rule, partly as a result of internal factionalism and partly because of pressure arising from militancy, terrorism and pressure from New Delhi. Even when presidential rule has not officially been imposed in Punjab, there has been a tendency since 1980 to rule it directly from New Delhi as a 'trouble state'.[1] Punjab conflict is best seen as a political conflict that has been transformed itself into a fratricidal or ethnic warfare. However, three somewhat different interpretations are also given to Punjab problem :

First, there has been a tendency in some of the literature to hold Indira Gandhi personally responsible for Punjab's political turmoil. There have been several variations on that theme : (1) Indira Gandhi was an indecisive leader who repeatedly failed to to negotiate a settlement with the Akali leadership during 1980-84. (2) Indira Gandhi was a Machiavellian leader who created a crisis because she wanted to 'save' India and thus win the next national election.[2] (3) Indira Gandhi was a power-hungry leader who repeatedly overcentralized the Indian polity and thus gave rise to numerous perverse center-state conflicts, including the one involving Punjab.[3] The last of these three is the most persuasive, because it best fits the evidence. However, an important objection can be raised to all of the explanations that blame Indira Gandhi. Whatever Indira Gandhi did, she did to many states, not only to Punjab. Why, then, should Punjab have experienced more turmoil than most other Indian states?

A second line of thinking on Punjab tends to put the blame on the Sikhs.[4] Again, there have been several variations on the theme : (1) The marriage of religion and politics in Sikhism has created real problems for democratic accommodation of a 'nationalist' conflict (2) Factionalism within the Akali party has made it difficult to find significant Sikh leaders with whom to negotiate. (3) The Sikh community is bent on imposing its will on the Hindus. Elements of these themes, especially those concerning factionalism within the Akali party, will be incorporated into a fuller explanation. The marriage of religion and politics, factionalism among the Akalis, and the power urge of the Sikhs as a community have all been around for quite sometime, but the violence and the governmental breakdown have been serious only during the past decade.

A third line of thought that appears to be more sensitive to the issue of socio-economic changes seeks to isolate the economic origins of the conflict. That argument points to the economic differentiation among the Sikhs, especially in the aftermath of the Green Revolution. Given these new economic differences, and the resulting antipathies, it was difficult for the Akali leadership to mobilize all the Sikhs to press even relatively innocuous community demands. The escalation of militancy and the mounting separatist demands should thus be seen from the standpoint of an attempt to create political unity in a class-divided ethnic community. But these economic variables cannot be considered decisive because the patterns of economic differentiation in neighbouring states like Haryana are not all that different from those in Punjab. If class conflicts deriving from the Green Revolutions, why are similar consequences not evident in Haryana?[5]

The origins of Punjab's complex and tragic civil disorder can be traced to the political conflict between Indira Gandhi and the Akali Dal.[6] In many respects, Indira Gandhi's attempts to keep the Akalis out of power after 1980, and the Akalis' repeated attempts to win back Punjab, constituted a 'normal' political conflict. That power struggle involving the Center and a regional party was not all that unusual. Indira Gandhi tried to maneuver several regional parties out of power in states such as West Bengal and Andhra Pradesh.

A number of factors, made the political struggle in Punjab especially explosive. The first was that Punjab was relatively evenly divided between the Sikhs and the Hindus, a situation virtually unique among India's states. Second, the close linkage of religion and politics in Sikhism made it difficult for the Akalis to search for political support outside the Sikh community. Four other variables contributed to the turmoil : (1) the weakness of the Akali Dal as a party; (2) some egregious political errors by Indira Gandhi such as her support of the militant religious preacher Bhindaranwale and the military assault on the Golden Temple; (3) a number of socio-economic conditions, such as the economic differentiations among the Sikhs, and their greater political impact because of their increasing wealth, and (4) the presence of large number of educated but unemployed Sikh youths.[7]

Prior to the political turmoil that arose in the 1980s caste and community divisions in Punjab had given rise to easily identifiable political divisions. In the past, the Hindus generally had supported the Congress Party, though a significant minority had been loyal to the Jan Sangh. The Akali Dal, by contrast, had consistently counted on the Sikh vote, but seldom had succeeded in mobilizing all the Sikhs as an ethnic political entity. The Jats, especially in the southern districts, had provided the main power base for the Akalis in Punjab. The Majhabis, however had seldom voted for the Akalis. Motivated by both caste and class animosities towards their employers, the Jat farmers, the Majhabis had tended to support either Congress or the leftist parties. The Bhapa Sikhs had also been politically divided. Many of them had resented their loss of the Akali leadership in the 1960s to the up-and-coming Green Revolution Jats. Some of the urban Sikhs had formerly supported Congress, and others, the Akali Dal.

Given all these basic divisions, Congress, during the 1960s and 1970s, often had been in a position to form a government in Punjab with the help of Hindus, Majhabi Sikhs, and urban Khatri Sikhs. The Akalis, by contrast, could form only a coalition government and that only with the pro-Hindu Jan Sangh. These political and community divisions provide the background essential for understanding the intensified political activities of the Akalis over the past decade. That militancy was aimed at mobilizing as many Sikhs as possible around a platform of 'Sikh nationalism'. The Akali Dal as a political party has always exhibited a mixture of religious fervor and hard-nosed political realism aimed at capturing power.[8]

The experience of the Akalis in and outside of the government during 1967-71 had some important political consequences. The fact that the Akalis were in alliance with the Jan Sangh tended to soften both the pro-Sikh communal edge of the Akalis and the pro-Hindu stance of the Jan Sangh. Thus, the more extreme communal elements among both the Hindus and the Sikhs became available for political mobilization. Congress sought to incorporate both of these extreme groups. The Congress strengthened its alliances with pro-Hindu groups, the more Congress in Punjab came to take on a communal hue similar to that of the Jan Sangh.[9] However, in a peculiar twist that revealed electoral opportunism run amok, Congress also encouraged the more extreme Sikh factions within the Akali Dal to break away from their party. Congress's temporary success on that front (e.g. the Lakshmi Singh Gill incident) succeeded in toppling the Akali government in the late 1960s. When that did not last, and the Akalis again formed a ruling coalition, the game of overthrowing the government continued, leading up to the imposition presidential rule in 1972.

That series of machinations by Congress made it clear to the Akalis that Congress leaders would go to great lengths to secure power in Punjab : If the Akalis could mobilize Sikh support around pro-Sikh issues. Congress was just as capable of playing the communal game to achieve political ends.

While Congress and the Akalis continued to mobilize and countermobilize, using any means at their disposal, including instigation of religious warfare, Punjabi society had been undergoing important changes.[10] Because of the increasing wealth of the Jat farmers, their donations to the gurudwaras, and thus the financial empire of the SGPC, rose enormously. That increased the ability of the Sikhs to launch and sustain political movements. Increasing personal wealth also led to rapid changes in life-styles. Growing consumerism, for example, threatened the cherished Sikh religious values of simplicity and asceticism. That opened the way for the more orthodox religious leaders to spread their message. The Sikh religion was in danger and had to be defended aggressively.[11] Increasing incomes and expenditures on consumer products and brought communications technology, such as tape recorders, to many Punjabi villages, and the recorded teachings of militant preachers like Bhindaranwale spread rapidly.

What finally precipitated conflict were political changes that came after 1980. It was in that year that the Janata party disintegrated nationally, and Indira Gandhi returned to power with a sizable majority. She went on to dismiss many of the state governments controlled by the opposition and to call for new state elections. The Akalis lost power in that national shuffle for the third time in a little over a decade. That must have left them with a bitter sense of having repeatedly been wronged by Indira Gandhi and Congress. In the 1980 state elections, however, the Akalis won only 27 percent of the popular vote. That must have confirmed for Indira Gandhi that she indeed had a right to dismiss an elected government and to call new elections.

She decided to use her position of advantage to launch a political offensive and consolidate her position vis-a-vis the Akalis. If she could use Bhindaranwale to split the ranks of the Akalis still further between the moderates and the extremists, victory would be hers. Her support for Bhindaranwale in 1981 and 1982 — the period when she enjoyed considerable political advantage over the Akalis in terms of popular support.

Both Indira Gandhi and the Akalis assembled militant forces for political ends. Over the next several years, the militancy led to civil disorder that took on a political life of its own, increasingly out of the control of both the Akalis and the national government. Whether that simply was not foreseen or was ignored under the short term pressure to seize political advantage may never be known. However, Bhindaranwale turned against Congress, which had encouraged him and helped him to become something of a cult hero. As a result, Bhindaranwale began to cultivate his own following. During 1981 and 1982, Bhindaranwale increasingly took advantage of his popularity to severe his links with Congress and to enlarge his political base. The repeated failure of the Akalis to wrest power from Congress had left them with the argument that increased militancy was the only means for protecting Sikh interests.

As Bhindaranwale's popularity soared, the Akalis launched their own 'dharm yudh' or holy war in 1982. That movement was aimed at mobilizing Sikhs to force the national government to accede to a series of demands, many of which had been spelled out in the Anandpur Sahib Resolution[12] of 1973 — such as the transfer of Chandigarh to Punjab, readjustment of irrigation allocation for some river waters, and an extension of the SGPC's control to the gurudwaras outside Punjab.

The failure of the negotiations between Indira Gandhi and the Akalis during 1982-84 marked an important turning point in the development of the Punjab conflict. It was during these two crucial years that the repeated inability to reach an agreement weakened the hold of the more moderate Sikh leaders over the regional nationalist movement.

The Akalis had never been a united lot. Their three prominent leaders, Badal, Tohra, and Longowal, came together during that period to bargain with Indira Gandhi, but they also fought with each other, jockeying for position within the party. Militancy, however, increasingly came to have its own dynamism. Bhindaranwale continued to be the tacit leader of those willing to employ open violence to achieve the goal of greater autonomy for the Sikhs, including a more specific goal of some elements : the creation of a sovereign state of Khalistan. The militants naturally were met with repression, which, combined with the charged appeals to religious nationalism, gave rise to further conflict. The frightened Hindus joined the Congress, strenghthening its political base. The Akalis thus found themselves being squeezed out of the political process, by the militant Sikhs on one side and by Indira's Congress on the other.

This highly condensed account of those complex events makes two things clear : First, the driving force behind the conflict was a power struggle between Indira's Congress and the Akali Dal. Both Sikh nationalism and the increasing militancy are better understood as products rather than as source of the power struggle. Second, because of the failure to achieve a negotiated settlement during 1982-84, the leadership of the movement began to pass out of the hands of those who basically wanted to win election paving the way for militant forces to take control over the political affairs of the state.

The repeated failure of negotiations between Indira and the Akali leaders continued to swell the ranks of the militants throughout 1983 and 1984. Under Bhindaranwale's tacit leadership, many of them began using gurdwaras as sancturies. The prominent leaders eventually made the Golden Temple, the most important of the Sikh gurudwaras, their base of operations. Thus, the movement for Sikh autonomy increasingly came to resemble a theorocratic fundamentalist movement, complete with its own 'ayatollahs' and zealous armed followers. Planned murders, as well as indiscriminate killings, continued to multiply. Hindus were killed by the militants so as to put pressure on the Congress government. Sikhs were killed so as to minimize dissent within the community. It was that atmosphere that led to the imposition of Presidential rule and later to a military assualt on the Golden Temple itself. The Operation Blue Star and the subsequent events, including the assassination of Indira Gandhi by her own Sikh bodyguards and massacre of large number of Sikhs in New Delhi and other places further added fuel to the Khalistan movement making democratic politics in the state of Punjab unworkable.

By the time Rajiv Gandhi took over the reigns of power Punjab had become the most important political issue in India. Within six months after coming to power in a Land slide electoral victory, Rajiv Gandhi, adapting a politically reconciliatary approach signed a negotiated agreement with the Akalis in that Rajiv gave in to virtually all the demands that his mother had rejected during early 1980s. The accord was put together in haste without enough consideration of the enormous complexity of issues involved. It did not address the issue of how to assuage the Sikhs sense of having been treated unjustly. This is not to suggest that the Rajiv-Longowal Accord of July 1985 was not a major step in the direction of discovering a democratic solution to the problem of Punjab. The accord failed to resolve the Punjab problem.

It was agreed in the accord to transfer Chandigarh to Punjab, to readjust some river irrigation waters in favor of Punjab, and to widen the scope of the inquiry into the killings of Sikhs in New Delhi.[13] With those major demands of the Akalis met, the way was clear to resume a more normal political process. It was obvious that after years of turmoil, normalcy would not easily return to Punjab. And yet simultaneously it was clear that holding elections and handing power over to the Akalis was the best way, if not the only way, to begin a long-term restoration of orderly government. That was certainly the new government's understanding. Thus, even Longowal's assassination by terrorist did not lead to postponement of state elections. Inspite of various obstacles, the elections went off peacefully, and as expected, the Akalis emerged victorious. The turnout for the elections was extremely high, nearly 70 per cent of the Punjab electorate, which was higher than that in either of the preceding state elections (1977 and 1980). Considering the difficult conditions within Punjab in the presence of a boycott call given by terrorists the participation rate must be viewed as a rejection of the more extreme demand (e.g., for Khalistan) and of the extraconstitutional political strategies adopted by the militants. The resumption of the political process led to a remarkable decline in terrorism.

Early attempts by the Rajiv government to restore democratic political order in Punjab were not sustained. The failure undermined the position of the Akali government, encouraged terrorism, and paved the way for the militants to assume positions of political prominence. The Akalis formed a government in Punjab under Barnala's leadership in October 1985. Within the first three months of his rule, Barnala found himself politically pressed on several sides. His most immediate problem was the factionalized leadership of his own party. What made the situation especially precarious for Barnala were two other contextual variables : a renewal of terrorism, and failure of the Rajiv Government to implement the accord.

The date announced for the transfer of Chandigarh to Punjab was January 26, 1986. It was not clear until the last minute that crucial clause of the accord would not be implemented. The Barnala government even issued invitations to celebrate the transfer. On the evening of January 25, however, word reached Chandigarh that the date of transfer had been postponed to March. When the March date came and went without the transfer of Chandigarh, it was clear that the Rajiv government had reneged on its agreement. Once that decision was made, much of the Punjab accord was doomed. The more it became clear that crucial clauses of the accord were not going to be implemented, the more pressed Barnala felt politically within Punjab. Barnala's approval rating depended heavily on his continuing capacity to elicit benefits for Punjab from New Delhi. New Delhi's failure to implement the accord weakened Barnala. As a result, both factionalism among the Akali leaders and terrorism intensified. The political approach slowly gave way to law and order approach or use of force approach.

As the law-and-order approach failed to bring terrorism under control, many competing groups with unclear goals began to crop up. Some of those groups proclaimed their goal to be the creation of a sovereign state of Khalistan, and to that end they were willing to kill as many Hindus as necessary to drive all Hindus out of Punjab. Other groups were less clear about their eventual goals. They sought to avenge what they perceived to be the insults visited on the Sikhs by New Delhi. Militant groups of both types were willing to kill not only Hindus but also other Sikhs. Continuing terrorism and rampant factionalism among the Akalis further weakened the Barnala government. Many of the Akali leaders were afraid of the terrrorists and simply refused to speak out against them. As the militants recongregated in the Golden Temple, Barnala also was forced to send in the police, thus further alienating many in the Sikh community.

Barnala's more militant rival, Tohra, won the elections to head the SGPC, thus demonstrating the growing political significance of the militants. The newly appointed militant priests even sought to dislodge Barnala from his position. Barnala's government survived, but only with the support of Congress legislators. Barnala had been reduced to a token leader in Punjab, kept on in power by New Delhi. By contrast, the religious organizations that underpinned the power of the Akali party increasingly came under the control of the militants. Rajiv finally dismissed the Barnala government and imposed Presidential rule on Punjab in May 1987.

The imposition of presidential rule did not make much difference for the everyday processes of government in Punjab. Terrorism continued, and many of the militants were again operating out of the Golden Temple. The situation in mid-1988 increasingly came to resemble that prevailing before Operation Blue Star in 1984, when presidential rule had been in effect and the terrorists had been in control of the Golden Temple. The Akalis had lost virtually all credibility by 1988. The militants, by contrast, were the only force with whom the government could deal. All this encouraged factional conflicts within the Akali party, further legitimised the militants and discredited the moderate Akali leaders and rendered elected governments ineffective and weak in the eyes of public and militants as well. This all turned Punjab into a testimony to India's growing problems of governability.

Due to the failure of the Government of India to continue its political approach towards the resolution of Punjab problem adopted by Rajiv Gandhi when he took over the reigns of power in a landslide electoral victory in 1985 the violence in the state continued unabated only to be combated by harsh security measures involving army, para-military forces and other law enforcing agencies of the state. Punjab after over a decade of violence appear to move towards the normalcy paving the way for political process to be initiated.

General Assembly elections were held in 1992. However flawed and skewed the general perception about the election was that atleast, there was recommencement of the political process as opposed to an imposed and adhoc governance. Elections were boycotted by Akalis. This resulted in the loss of Akali Dal to reassert its political and organisational relevance in the state of Punjab, thereby helping the Congress to re-emerge on the political scene of Punjab where its presence had almost become extinct.

This initiation of political process gradually progressed towards more stable and normal existence. Though the initiation of political process helped in bringing militancy and violence to normalcy but it was not completely crushed or suppressed or died down. Sporadic incidence of violence continued. Militant continue to regroup themselves to make their presence felt by resorting to violence. The assassination of Mr. Beant Singh, Congress Chief Minister of Punjab in 1996, recent explosion in a train and the plantation of a bomb in a Hindu Temple are the pointers towards the point that militancy in Punjab can reemerge given the opportunity which exsisted during the last decade mainly as a result of power politics of Congress and Akali political parties.

References

1. Gurharpal Singh, 'Understanding the Punjab Problem', *Asian Survey*, December 1987, pp. 1268-1277.

2. Rajni Kothari and Giri Deshingkar, 'Punjab : The Longer View'. *Illustrated Weekly of India*, July 15, 1984, pp. 20-30; D.L. Sheth and A.S. Narang, 'The Electoral Angle', in Amrik Singh, (ed.), *Punjab in Indian Politics : Issues and Trends*, Ajanta Publication, Delhi 1985, pp. 123-35.

3. Paul Brass, 'The Punjab Crisis and the Unity of India', in Kohli, (ed.), *India's Democracy*, pp. 169-213.

4. Scholarly accounts generally shy away from assigning direct blame to the Sikhs. This theme, however is central to India's political discourse, as revealed in editorials in *Mainstream*, newspapers and political speeches by such right-wing Hindu party leaders as Bal Thackeray of the Shiv Sena.

5. Gopal Singh, 'Socio-economic Bases of Punjab Crisis', *Economic and Political Weekly*, January 7,1984, pp. 42-46, and H.K. Puri, 'Akali Agitation : An Analysis of the Socio-Economic Basic of Protest', *Economic and Political Weekly*, January 22,1983 pp. 113-19.

6. I.K. Gujaral, 'The Sequence', Seminar, February 1984, pp. 14-17; Gian Singh Sandhu' 'The Roots of the Problem', in Amrik Singh, n. 2,pp. 61-70, Sucha Singh Gill and K.C. Singhal, 'The Punjab Problem : Its Historical Roots', *Economic and Political Weekly*, April 7, 1984, pp. 603-608.

7. Amrik Singh, 'An Approach to the Problem', in Amrik Singh, n. 2, pp. 2-10.

8. Khushwant Singh, *A History of the The Sikhs*, 1839-1964, vol. II, Princeton University Press, 1966, Parts IV and V, Rajiv A. Kapur, Sikh Separatism : *The Politics of Faith*, Allen and Unwin, London, 1986, especially Chapters 4-7 : Baldev Raj Nayar, *Minority Politics in the Punjab*, Princeton University press, 1966; A.S. Narang, *Storm over the Sutlej : Akali Politics* : Gitanjali

Publishing House, New Delhi, 1983; Mohinder Singh, *The Akali Movement*, Macmillan, Delhi 1978.

9. Gill and Singhal, n. 6, pp. 606-607.

10. Robin Jeffery, *What's Happening to India ? : Punjab, Ethnic Conflict, Mrs. Gandhi's Death and the Test for Federalism*, Macmillan, Basingtoke, 1986.

11. Joyce Pettingrew, 'In Search of New Kingdom of Lahore', *Pacific Affairs*, Spring 1987, pp. 1-25.

12. See Appendix-A.

13. See Appendix-B.

5

Conclusion

Punjab underwent a decade of militancy and violence due to combination of various reasons and causes. This problem was the progeny of socio-economic-politico-religious factors, having roots both in pre-and post-independence history of India.

Sikh religion considers politics as inseparable part of it. More so, militancy was injected into it since the days of Guru Gobind Singh. The religious identity was exploited by the Britishers to give them political identity. It was also used for political expediency even after independence. The problems of Sikhs were not properly attended and settled. The issue of their language and Sikh dominated state were highly politicised to assume heavy communal overtones, giving birth to power politics in the state between Congress, Akali Dal and Jan Sangh.

Congress played the game of divide and rule with Sikh leadership. Sikh leadership in the process very effectively articulated Sikh grievances for political expediencey. Akali Dal (dominated by rich Sikh peasantry) remained somewhat restrained when in power as party of various coalitions and became communal when in opposition. The same was true to some extent of the Congress. The political patronage given to a fundamentalist Sant Bhindaranwale with the intention of dividing the Akali leadership boomranged. Thereby encouraging Sikh extremism and militancy.

Such a role of Congress in the state continuously eroded the moderate Sikh leadership resulting into violence and militancy on the one hand increasing fragmentation of Sikh politics and the virtual breakdown of state government as well on the other hand. The repeated impositions of President rules reflected the political stalemate and increasing involvement of the central government in the strife-ridden state of Punjab. In the process Sikh religiousity was imparted communal overtones by Akalis and Congress leadership for political mileage with extreme manifestation of this being the articulation of the urges of Sikhs to be recognised as distinct ethnic community and to enjoy political rights on that basis in their own rights, which gave birth to the demand of Khalistan.

This aggravated the communal divide in Punjab. While the Akali Dal did not oppose militancy, Jan Sangh demanded the use of army for curbing the growing violence. Similarly, the Akali Dal vehemently opposed operation Blue Star and other such actions undertaken by the Central government from time to time, Jan Sangh defended these steps with the result that both the communities Punjabis and Hindu acted and reacted from perceived positions as threatened minorities largely created by political elites for political expendiency. Sikh and Hindu identities as a consequnce became more salient than Punjabi or Indian identities.

The inability of the government to tackle the problem with a clear vision and understanding of the situation, its various dimensions and factors contributed to the growth of militancy and violence in the state. Government, infact, mishandled the problem right from the beginning. The strategy of the government was simply based on the use of force, which probably intended to vanish the terrorists not the causes which led to such choatic and violent situation in Punjab. The use of force strategy was not even well coordinated and executed. It was not learnt by the government of India from the experiences that nowhere repressive measures were successful in tackling the problem of militancy and terrorism.

The Punjab problem was not dealt properly with a clear political vision. Political ambitions of the then ruling party (Congress) in Delhi were of prime consideration for it than the national interests. Rajiv Gandhi after taking over the reigns of power attempted to resolve the conflict by signing an agreement with Akalis. He himself could not implement the agreement. This encouraged factional conflicts within Akali party, legitimised the militants, discredited the moderate Akali leaders and rendered the elected government weak and ineffective in the eyes of public and militants as well. This further contributed to the militancy and violence in Punjab only to be tackled with harsh security measures, paving the way for assembly elections in 1992. This was the commencement of a political process as opposed to an imposed and adhoc governance. This put Punjab on the track of stability and normalcy.

Punjab conflict was infact, a political conflict that had transferred itself into an ethnic warfare for an ethnic homeland. The driving force behind the Punjab problem was power struggle between Congress and Akali Dal. Sikh nationalism and militancy were the products rather than the source of power struggle. Due attention to the problems of Sikhs by the government would have hardly developed into such an explosive and emotive manifestation of the problem. Not only this, the power struggle also resulted into the weakening of the myriad political institutions and in the process decaying of them. Though the state of Punjab is back to normalcy sporadic incidence of violence are still continuing. Given the opportunity as existed during the beginning of the last decade the existing situation may again turn chaotic and turbulence.

Suggestions

The concept of a nation is the only universally recognised and internationally valid concept for the sovereign aggregate of human beings in modern state. If modern states are nation states or multinationality states, then the territorial integrity, political stability and the legitimacy of the state is predicted upon the political if not also emotional, integration of its citizens.

Plurality of Indian state exists in almost every aspect of its collective life-horizontally, sociologically, ethnically, culturally, linguistically, with multi-religions wide disparity of economic conditions as well as technology and finally ideologically (rightest, leftist and centrist). Vertically also our society is split between castes and sub-castes.

With such a deliberate social fabric India poses the problem that various stratas of the society do not accept the fact that we are a nation. Acceptance of this chief objective which needs sound governance, clean political life and effective institutions which are the prerequisites of insuring a dignified living.

Generation of the nationalism and building up of a standardized living requires a secure state i.e. a state which is territorially integrated, politically stable and legitimate state through good governance, proper organisation and functioning of the Government and its various agencies like Defence forces, police, bureaucracy, judisciary etc. Security (internal as well as external) of the nation is the consequence of a combined good efforts of all these governmental institutions. A close correlation exists between art of government, defence against external threats and protection against internal threats.

Thus the very first step towards the security of nation is the acceptance that we are one nation and there has to be institutionalised handling of national security both external and internal. This requires a sound centralised policy and planning and strong defence insfrastructure. An enlightened leadership is the need of hour, what we need is an integrated decision-making structure for long term planning (based on prevailing as well as perceived security threats in the environment) and not just ad-hoc decisions which is the current norm.

An efficient administration will be an effective instrument in itself paving way for national integration. There should be a political will to govern well and honestly. To handle internal security problems we need a viable policy, a sincere and credible approach and dedicated execution entirely dictated by national interest.

Right detection of internal security threats is equally important. Those with secessionist tendencies with or without external aid and which requires the extensive use of Armed forces as a counter-strategy. Another is those type of disorders which reflect the social tensions of the political system but with no secessionist tendencies which requires a right national policy and proper resource management.

All internal conflicts have small beginning—petty causes—for ex. Mizo trouble started from the Bamboo famine, in Punjab from the peasant discontentment with the electricity bound, and the Kashmiris trouble from fraudulent election. The negligence on the part of concerned government/its agencies proliferated them.

What we need is highly skilled task-oriented and result-oriented institutions which rely on fast and timely decisions with a fair perception of the environment. A complete coordination of all forces is essential. Different forces with a common target should have a similar outlook. Those with in-depth knowledge of terrain and people should first tackle the problem. An efficient intelligence is equally important.

A major lacunae of Indian security system is that the forces (police, paramilitary or army) is the lack of adequate training and resources and lack of proper coordination amongst them.

Besides, effective resource management be it national or human resource — is another indispensable ingredient of sound security system. In such a scenario, where the unity, integrity and security of a nation is threatened by its own constituents, only solution is that of — 'Domestic Social Cohesion'. A 'culture of accomodation', has to be developed between various antagonistic groups — a system of mutual give and take and cooperation is the need of hour. But enhancement of 'state capability' is the pre-requisite. 'State capability' does not simply mean the military capability rather in view of renewed definition of 'Security' whereby it is more a phenomenon of domestic factors/forces, state capability is to be measured in terms of industrial, economic strength and political alliances. World today is giving primacy to such non-political issues of security. Simultaneously the process of nation-building has to be strengthened so that parochial affinities of region, religion, caste, ethnicity and tribal relentities no more carry the potential to be mis-utilised by anti-national or vested interests for their gains, endangering the national security.

Security aspects, domestic politics and global politics are highly inter-related. On account of 'Globalisation of world economies', any happening in any party of the world is going to effect rest. Any global development that may sensitize any part of our delicate social fabric has to be taken due care of by the political elite.

History of modernisation and development is highly influenced by the western legacy which is an example of intensive labour and long struggle on this part. Countries of the developed world really did a lot to create a highly strong social infrastructure of health, education, family welfare, women empowerment etc. So, giving platitudes is not enough but an intesive labour and active participation is required to make the country really secure as dangers to our security are more domestic in nature and origin.

Appendix - A

Anandpur Sahib Resolution 1977

Anandpur Sahib Resolution 1977

May the Panth Prevail • May the victory by ever with the Panth

Foreword

the Shiromani Akali Dal undoubtedly, is a great organisation whose coming into existence has been a matter of pride for the Sikhs. Its entire history is a glorious record of struggles and agitations, victories and achievements of which it can be justly proud of. The past record of the party vouchsafes that whoever has ever tried to confront it, he did have to perish ultimately. The most momentous party played by it in the Freedom Struggle of the country would ever form an indelible party of history written in letters of gold.

Shiromani Akali Dal has been guiding the Sikhs according to exigencies of the situation for their rights and for a respectable status in the set-up of the country. Its objective has been exaltation of the Sikh Panth and for the achievement of this lofty ideal Shiromani Akali Dal has been adopting different and varied means.

Keeping in view the anti-Sikh policies of the Congress government and the political, social and economic conditions pulsating in the country, the Shiromani Akali Dal has decided to redraw the aims and objectives of the Sikhs Panth and to give a more vigorous lead for their achievements so that by so doing it may serve the larger interests of the Panth, the Punjab as also the Country and thus live upto the expectations of the Sikhs.

For such a purpose, a sub-committee of the Sikh intellectuals and thinkers was formed by the Shiromani Akali Dal at a meeting of its Working Committee held on 11-12-1972 to draw up the draft of a 'Policy Programme' with the General Secretary of the Party, S. Surjit Singh Barnala, as its Chairman, and S. Gurcharan Singh Tohra, M.P., President, Shiromani Gurudwara Parbandhak Committee, Jathedar Jiwan Singh Umranangal, S. Gurmit Singh, ex-Minister, Dr. Bhagat Singh, ex-Minister, S. Balwant Singh, ex-Finance Minister, S. Jaswinder Singh Brar, General Secretary, Shiromani Akali Dal, S. Bhag Singh, ex-M.L.A., Major General Gurbux Singh Badhni and S. Amar Singh Ambalvi, Advocate, as its members.

This Sub-Committee had eleven sittings beginning with the first at Amritsar, on 23-12-1972. Most of the meetings were held at Chandigarh for its peaceful and congenial atmosphere.

All the members of the sub-committee evinced keen interest in its working and engaged themselves in very interesting and useful discussion which were a treat to watch and partake of. A unanimous report was ultimately drawn up after very close deliberations on each and every aspect of the matters and more subtle of their aspects. Actuated by feelings of love for the Sikh Panth, more of its eminent Army Generals. Legal experts, Doctors, Political thinkers, experienced politicians and religious leaders joined together to lend thier helping hands to draw up this plan for a more glorious future of the Panth. During their discussions a very happy balance of love for the Panth and the Country was all too evident, as also the keenness to safeguard the interests of the Sikhs and the Country.

When the meticulously drawn up report of S. Surjit Singh Sub-committee was presented in the meeting of the Working

Committee of Shiromani Akali Dal held at Shri Anandpur Sahib, the sacred and historic seat of the Tenth Lord, it was approved, after close discussions extending over two days, for placing it before the General House.

This draft is, therefore, being sent to you to enable you to study it in depth so that the meeting of the General House may be benefited by your valued opinion.

With Panthic Love and regards.

Office of	Yours humbly,
Shiromani Akali Dal,	AJMER SINGH
Sri Amritsar	Secretary
1.8.1977.	Shiromani Akali Dal

THE RESOLUTIONS

adopted, in the light of the Anandpur Sahib Resolution, at the open session of the 18th All India Akali Conference held at Ludhiana on 28-29 October, 1978 under the Presidentship of Jathedar Jagdev Singh Talwandi are as under :

(It was after the passing of these Resolutions that the Shiromani Akali Dal started the struggle therefor).

Resolution No.1

Moved by S. Gurcharan Singh Tohra, President Shiromani Gurudwara Parbandhak Committee and endorsed by S. Parkash Singh Badal, Chief Minister, Punjab.

This Shiromani Akali Dal realizes that India is a federal and republican geographical entity of different languages, religions and cultures. To safeguard the fundamental rights of the religious and linguistic minorities, to fulfil the demands of the democratic traditions and to pave the way for economic progress, it has become imperative that the

Indian constitutional infrastructure should be given a real federal shape by redefining the central and state relations and rights on the lines of the aforesaid principles and objectives.

The concept of total revolution given by Lok Naik, Sh. Jayaprakash Narain is also based upon the progressive decentralization of powers The climax of the process of centralization of powers of the states through repeated amendments of the Constitution during the Congress regime came before the countrymen in the form of the Emergency, when all fundamental rights of all citizens were usurped. It was then that the programme of decentralization of powers ever advocated by Shiromani Akali Dal was openly accepted and adopted by other political parties including Janata Party, C.P.I. (M), A.D.M.K. etc.

Shiromani Akali Dal has ever stood firm on this principle and that is why after very careful consideration it unanimously adopted a resolution to this effect first at all India Akali Conference, Batala, then at Sri Anandpur Sahib which has endorsed the principle of State autonomy in keeping with the concept of Federalism.

. As such, the Shiromani Akali Dal emphatically urges upon the Janata Government to take cognizance of the different linguistic and cultural sections, religious minorities as also the voice of millions of people and recast the constitutional structure of the country on real and meaningful federal principles to obviate the possibility of any danger to National unity and the integrity of the country and further, to enable the states to play a useful role for the progress and prosperity of the Indian people in their respective areas by the meaningful exercise of their powers.

Resolution No.2

The momentous meeting of the Shiromani Akali Dal calls upon the Government of India to examine carefully the long tale of the excesses, wrongs, illegal actions committed by the previous Congress government, more particularly during Emergency, and try to find an early solution to the following problems :

(a) Chandigarh originally raised as a Capital for Punjab should be handed over to Punjab.

(b) The long standing demand of the Shiromani Akali Dal for the merger in Punjab of the Punjabi-speaking areas, to be identified by linguistic experts with village as a unit, should be conceded.

(c) The control of Head Works should continue to be vested in Punjab and, if need be, the Reorganisation Act should be amended.

(d) The arbitrary and unjust Award given by Mrs. Indira Gandhi during the Emergency on the distribution of Ravi-Beas waters should be revised on the universally accepted norms and principles, thereby justice be done to Punjab.

(e) Keeping in view the special aptitude the martial qualities of the Sikhs the present ratio of their strength in Army should be maintained.

(f) The excesses being committed on the settlers in the Tarai region of U.P. in the name of Land Reforms should be vacated by making suitable amendments in the Ceiling Law on the Central guidelines.

Resolution No.3

(Economic Policy Resolution)

The chief sources of inspiration of the economic policies and programme of the Shiromani Akali Dal are the secular, democratic and socialistic concepts of Sri Nanak Dev and Sri Guru Gobind Singh Ji. Our Economic programme is based on three basic principles :

(a) Dignity of Labour

(b) An economic and social structure which provides for the uplift of the poor and depressed sections of society.

(c) Unabated opposition to concentration of economic and political power in the hands of the capitalists.

While drafting its economic policies and programme, the Shiromani Akali Dal in its historic Anandpur Sahib resolution has laid particular stress on the need to break the monopolistic hold of the capitalists foisted on the Indian economy by 30 years of Congress rule in India. This capitalist hold enabled the central government to assume all powers in its hands after the manner of Mughal Imperialism. This was bound to thwart the economic progress of the states and injure the social and economic interests of the people. The Shiromani Akali Dal once again reiterates the Sikh way of life by resolving to fulfil the holy words of Guru Nanak Dev :

'He alone realizes the Truce Path who labours honestly and shares the fruits of that Labour'.

This way of life is based upon three basic principles :

(i) Doing honest labour,

(ii) Sharing the fruits of this labour, and

(iii) Meditation on the Lord's Name.

The Shiromani Akali Dal calls upon the Central and the State governments to eradicate unemployment during the next ten years. While pursuing this aim, special emphasis should be laid on ameliorating the lot of the weaker sections, scheduled and depressed classes, workers, landless and poor farmers and urban poor. Minimum wages should be fixed for them all.

The Shiromani Akali Dal urges upon the Punjab Government to draw up such an economic plan for the State as would turn it into the leading province during the next ten years, by raising per capita income to Rs. 3,000 and by generating an economic growth rate of 7% per annum as against 4% at National Level.

The Shiromani Akali Dal gives first priority to the redrafting of the taxation structure in such a way that the burden of taxation is shifted from the poor to the richer classes and an equitable distribution of National income is ensured.

The main plank of the economic programme of the Shiromani Akali Dal is to enable the economically weaker sections of the Society to share the fruits of National income.

The Shiromani Akali Dal calls upon the Central Government to make an international air-field at Amritsar which should also enjoy the facilities of a dry part. Similarly, a Stock Exchange should be opened at Ludhiana to accelerate the process of industrialization and economic growth in the State. The Shiromani Akali Dal also desires that suitable amendments should be made in the Foreign Exchange rules for free exchange of foreign currencies and thereby removing the difficulties being faced by the Indian emigrants.

The Shiromani Akali Dal emphatically urges upon the Indian Government to bring a parity between the prices of the agricultural produce and that of the industrial raw materials so that the discrimination against such states which lack these materials may be removed.

The Shiromani Akali Dal demands that the exploitation of the producers of the cash crops like cotton, sugarcane, oil seeds etc. at the hands of the traders should be stopped forthwith and for such a purpose arrangements for the purchase of these crops by the government, at remunerative prices, should be made. Besides, effective steps should be taken by the government for the purchase of cotton through the Cotton Corporation.

The Shiromani Akali Dal strongly feels that the most pressing National problem is the need to ameliorate the lot of millions of exploited persons belonging to the scheduled classes. For such a purpose the Shiromani Akali Dal calls upon the Central and State Governments to earmark special funds. Besides, the State Governments should allot sufficient funds in their respective budgets for giving free residential plots both in the urban and rural areas to the scheduled castes.

The Shiromani Akali Dal also calls for the rapid diversification of farming. The shortcomings in the Land Reforms Laws should be removed, rapid industrialization of the State ensured, the credit facilities for the medium industries expanded and unemployment allowance given to those who are unemployed. For remunerative farming, perceptible reduction should be made on the prices of farm machinery like tractors, tube-wells as also the inputs, etc.

Resolution No.4

This huge session of the Shiromani Akali Dal regrets the discrimination to which the Punjabi language is being subjected in the adjoining States of Himachal, Haryana, Delhi and Jammu and Kashmir, etc. It is its firm demand that in accordance with the Nehru Language Formula, the neighbouring States of Punjab should be 'given second' language status to the Punjabi language because a fairly large sections of their respective population are Punjabi-speaking.

Resolution No.5

The meeting regrets that against the 'claims' of the refugees who had migrated to Jammu and Kashmir as a result of the partition of the country, no compensation has been provided to them even after such a long time and these unfortunate refugees are rotting in the camps ever since then.

This Akali Dal Session, therefore, forcefully demands that their claims should be soon settled and immediate steps should be taken to rehabilitate them even if it involves an amendment in Section 370.

Resolution No.6

The 18th Session of the All India Akali Conference takes strong exceptions to the discrimination to which the minorities in other states are being subjected and the way in which their interests are being ignored.

As such, it demands that injustice against the Sikhs in other states should be vacated and proper representation should be given to them in the government service, local bodies, state legislatures, through nomination if need be.

Resolution No.7

The 18th Session of the All India Akali Conference notes with satisfaction that mechanization of farming in the country has led to increase in the farm yield and as a result the country is heading towards self-sufficiency.

However, the session feels that poor farmers are unable to take to mechanization because of the enormity of the cost involved.

As such, the Shiromani Akali Dal urges upon the Government of India to abolish the excise duty on tractors so that with the decrease in their prices the ordinary farmers may also be to avail of farm machinery and contribute to the growth of gross agricultural produce of the country.

Resolution No.8

The meeting of the Shiromani Akali Dal appeals to the Central and State Governments to pay particular attention to the poor and labouring classes and demands that besides making suitable amendments in the Minimum Wages Act, suitable legal steps should be taken to improve the economic lot of the labouring class to enable it to lead a respectable life and play a useful role in the rapid industrialization of the country.

Resolution No.9

This session seeks permission from the Government of India to instal a broadcasting station at Golden Temple, Amritsar, for the relay of 'Gurbani Kirtan' for the spiritual satisfaction of those Sikhs who are living in foreign lands.

The session wishes to make it clear that the entire cost of the proposed Broadcasting Project would be borne by the Khalsa Panth and its over-all control shall vest with the Indian Government. We have every hope that the government would have no hesitation in conceding this demand after due consideration.

Resolution No.10

The huge Session of the Shiromani Akali Dal strongly urges upon the Government of India to make necessary amendments in the following enactments for the benefits of the agricultural classes who have toiled hard for the larger National interests :

1. By suitable amendment in the relevant clause of the Hindu Succession Act, a woman should be given

rights of inheritance in the properties of her father-in-laws instead of the father's.

2. The agricultural lands of the farmers should be completely exempted from the Wealth Tax and the Estate Duty.

Resolution No.11

The vast Session of the Shiromani Akali Dal strongly impresses upon the Government of India that keeping in view the economic backwardness of the scheduled and non-scheduled castes provisions proportionate to their population should be made in the budget for utilization for their welfare. A special ministry should be created at the centre as a practical measure to render justice to them on the basis of reservation.

The Session also calls upon the government that in keeping with the settlement already no discrimination should be made between the Sikh and Hindu Harijans in any part of the country.

Resolution No.12

The Congress government is called upon to vacate the gross injustice, discrimination done to Punjab in the distribution of Ravi-Beas waters. The Central Government must also give approval for the immediate establishment of six sugar and four textile mills in Punjab so that the state may be able to implement its agro-industrial policy.

Basic Postulates Of The Shiromani Akali Dal

As adopted by the Working Committee of the Shiromani Akali Dal at its meeting held at Sri Aanadpur Sahib on 16-!7 October, 1973.

(A) Postulates

1. The Shiromani Akali Dal is the very embodiment of the hopes and aspirations of the Sikh Nation and as such is fully entitled to its representation. The basic postulates of this organisation are Human Co-existence, Human progress and ultimate unity of all Human beings with the Spiritual Soul.

2. These postulates are based upon the three great principles of Sri Guru Nanak Dev ji, namely, a Meditation on God's Name, dignity of labour and sharing of fruits of this Labour.

(Nam Japo, Kir at Karo, Wand Chhako)

(B) Purposes

The Shiromani Akali Dal shall ever strive to achieve the following aims :

1. Propagation of Sikhism and its code of conduct denounciation of atheism.
2. To preseve and keep alive the concept of distinct and independent identity of the Panth and to create an environment in which national sentiments and aspirations of the Sikhs Panth will find full expression, satisfaction and growth.
3. Eradication of poverty and Starvation, by increased production and more equitable distribution of wealth and the establishment of a just social order sans any exploitation.
4. Vacation of discrimination on the basis of caste, creed or illiteracy in keeping with basic principles of Sikhism.
5. Striving for the removal of diseases and ill-health denouncement of use of intoxicants and enlargement

of facilities for physical well-being to prepare and enthuse the Nation for the National defence.

FIRST PART

The Shiromani Akali Dal considers it its primary duty to inculcate among the Sikhs, religious fervour and a pride in their rich religious heritage for which it proposes to pursue the following programme :

(a) Reiteration of the concept of the unicity (Oneness) of God, meditation on His Name, recitation of Gurbani, renewal of faith to the ten Holy Sikh Gurus and the Holy Sir Guru Granth Sahib and other appropriate measures for such a purpose.

(b) Grooming accomplished preachers, Ragis, Dhadis, and poets in the Sikhs Missionary College for a more effective propagation of Sikhism, Sikh Philosophy, belief in Sikh code of conduct and Kirtan etc., at home and abroad, in schools and colleges, in villages and in cities as indeed at every place.

(c) Baptising the Sikhs (Amrit Parchar) on a vast scale, with particular emphasis on Schools and Colleges of which the teachers and the taught shall be enthused through regular study circles.

(d) Reinculcate the religious practice of 'DASWAND' among the Sikhs. (Giving one-tenth of one's earnings for the welfare of the Community).

(e) Generating feelings of respect for the Sikh intellectuals, writers, Preachers, Granthis, etc., who also in turn, would be enthused to improve upon their accomplishments while conforming to the basic Sikh tenets and traditions.

(f) Streamlining the Gurudwaras administration by giving better training to their workers. Appropriate steps would also be taken to maintain Gurudwara buildings in proper condition. For such a purpose, the party representatives in the Shiromani Gurudwara Parbandhak Committee and local Committees would be directed from time to time to pull their weight.

(g) Making appropriate arrangemtns for the error free publication of Gurbani, promoting research work in the ancient and modern Sikh history as also its publication, rendering Gurbani in other languages and producing first rate literature on Sikhism.

(h) Taking appropriate steps for the enactment of an All India Gurudwara Act with a view to introduce improvements in the administration of the Gurudwaras throughout the country and to reintegrate the traditional preaching sects of Sikhism like Udasis and Nirmalas with the mainstream of Sikhism without in any way encroaching on the properties of their respective individual 'maths'.

(i) Taking such steps as may be necessary to bring the Sikh Gurudwaras all over the world under a single system of administration with a view to run them according to the basic Sikh norms and to pool their sources for the dissemination of Sikhism on a wider and more impressive scale.

(j) Striving for free access to all those holy Sikh Shrines, including Nankana Sahib from which the Sikh Panth has been separated for pilgrimage and proper upkeep.

Political Goal

The political goal of the Panth, without doubt, is enshrined in the commandments of the Tenth Lord, in the pages of the Sikh history and in the very heart of the Khalsa Panth, the ultimate objective of which is the pre-eminence of the Khalsa.

The fundamental policy of the Shiromani Akali Dal is to seek the realization of this birth right of the Khalsa through creation of congenial environment and a political set up.

For Attainment of This Aim

1. The Shiromani Akali Dal is determined to strive by all possible means to :

   (a) Have all those Punjabi-speaking areas, deliberately kept out of Punjab, such a Dalhousie in Gurdaspur District, Chandigarh, Pinjore-Kalka and Ambala Saddar etc., in Ambala District, the entire Una Tehsil of Hoshiarpur District, the 'Desh' area of Nalagarh, Shahabad and Gulha blocks of Karnal District, Tohana Sub-Tehsil, Ratia block and Sirsa Tehsil of Hissar District and six Tehsils of Ganga Nagar District in Rajasthan, merged with Punjab to constiute a single administrative unit where the interests of the Sikhs and Sikhism are specifically protected.

   (b) In this new Punjab and in other States the centre's interference would be restricted to Defence, Foreign relations, Currency and General Communication, all other departments would be in the jurisdiction of Punjab (and other states) which would be fully entitled to frame own Laws on these Subjects for administration. For the above departments of the Centre, Punjab and other States contribute in proportion to representation in the Parliament.

   (c) The Sikhs and other religious minorities living out of Punjab should be adequately protected against any kind of discrimination.

2. The Shiromani Akali Dal would also endeavour to have the Indian Constitution recast on real federal principles, with equal representation at the centre for all the States.

3. The Shiromani Akali Dal strongly denounces the foreign policy of India framed by the Congress party. It is worthless, hopeless and highly detrimental to the interests of the Country, the Nation and the Mankind at large. Shiromani Akali Dal shall extend its support only to that foreign policy of India which is based on the principles of Peace and National interests. It strongly advocates a policy of peace with all neighbouring countries, especially those inhabited by the Sikhs and their sacred shrines. The Akali Dal is of the firm view that our foreign policy should in no case play second fiddle to that of any other country.

4. The Shiromani Akali Dal shall raise its firm voice against any discrimination against any Sikh (or even other) employees of the Central or State Governments. The Shiromani Akali Dal shall also endeavour to maintain the traditional position of the Sikhs in all the wings of the defence departments and the Panth would pay particular attention to the needs of the Sikh Armymen. The Shiromani Akali Dal would also see that 'kirpan' is accepted as an integral part of the Uniform of the Sikhs in Army.

5. It shall be the primary duty of the Shiromani Akali Dal to help rehabilitate the ex-servicemen of the Defence Departments in the civil life and /or such a purpose it would extend them every help to enable them to organize themselves so that they are able to raise their voice in an effective way for gaining adequate concessions and proper safeguards for a life of self-respect and dignity.

6. The Shiromani Akali Dal is of the firm opinion that all those persons—males or females—who have not been convicted of any criminal offence by a court of law, should be at liberty to possess all types of small arms, like revolvers, guns, pistols, rifles, carbines etc., without any licence, the only obligation being their registration.
7. The Shiromani Akali Dal seeks ban on the sale of liquor and other intoxicants and shall press for prohibition on the consumption of intoxicants and smoking on public places.

The Economic Policy And Programme Of The Shiromani Akali Dal

As adopted by its Working Committee on 17th October, 1973 at its meeting held at Sri Anandpur Sahib.

Although the mainstay of the Indian economy is agriculture and all those political powers who claim to raise social structure on the basis of justice cannot afford to ignore this fact, yet this is a hard fact that the levels of economic powers, continue to be in the hands of big traders, capitalists and monopolists. Some marginal benefits might have accrued to other classes, but the real benefits of economic growth have been reaped by these categories during the last 26 years after Independence. The political power has also been misappropriated by these classes which are wielding the same for their own benefits. As such, any peaceful attempt to usher in a new era of social justice would have to break the economic and political strongholds of these categories of the people.

The Shiromani Akali Dal strongly advocates that the growing gulf between the rich and the poor, in the urban and rural areas both should be abridged but, it is of the firm opinion that, for such a purpose, the first assault would have to be made on the classes who have assumed all the reins of economic power in their hands. In rural areas, the Akali Dal determined to help the weaker classes, like the scheduled castes, backward classes, landless tenants, ordinary labourers, the poor and middle class farmers. For such a purpose, it stands for meaningful land reforms which envisage a ceiling of 30 standard acres and the distribution of excess land among the poor farmers.

The motto of the Shiromani Akali Dal is to provide employment for all, requisite food and clothing for all, a house to live in, suitable transport and to create means to fulfil all those necessities of a civilized life without which life appears incomplete.

As such, the economic policy of the Shiromani Akali Dal shall endeavour to achieve the following objectives :

Agriculture Sector

During recent years the agriculture sector has witnessed land reforms and green revolution. The Shiromani Akali Dal undertakes to enrich the green revolution by an increase in yield per acre. It shall also ensure perceptible improvement in the standard of living of all rural classes, more particulrly of the poor and the middle class farmers, as also the landless labourers. For such a purpose it plans to work on the following lines :

(a) Introducing land reforms and measures for increasing agricultural production with a view to remove the growing gap between the rich and the poor. For such a purpose the existing legislation on land ceiling would have to be revised and a firm ceiling of 30 standard acres per family would have to be enforced with proprietary rights to the actual tillers. The excess land would be distributed among the landless tenants and poor farmers, while the cultivable government land lying unused shall be distributed among the landless classes, especially the scheduled castes and tribes. While distributing such lands the interests of Harijan and Landless labourers would be particularly taken care of. The Akali Dal would also consider the possibilities of allowing the tenants to service loans by mortgaging land under their plough, as also prohibiting the scheduled castes/tribes and backward classes from mortgaging the land distributed among them.

(b) The Shiromani Akali Dal shall work for the modernization of farming and would also try to enable the middle class and poor farmers to seek loans and inputs made available by different agencies.

(c) The Shiromani Akali Dal shall try to fix the prices of the agricultural produce on the basis of the returns of the middle class farmers. Such prices would be notified well before the sowing season and only the State governments would be empowered to fix such prices.

(d) The Shiromani Akali Dal stands for complete nationalization of the trade in foodgrains and as such, shall endeavour to nationalize the wholesale trade in foodgrains through the establishment of State agencies.

(e) The Shiromani Akali Dal strongly oppose the demarcation of food zones and the attendant restrictions on the movements of the foodgrains. The whole country should be the single food zone.

The party shall make special efforts to bring the Thein Dam and the Bhatinda Thermal Plant to a speedy completion so that increased and cheaper power and irrigation facilities are available . Dessure efforts would be made for the establishment of an Atomic power station in the State.

Co-operative societies would be set up in the rural areas. In all those areas where canal water is not available small irrigation projects would be taken in hand.

Industrial Sector

The Shiromani Akali Dal strongly advocates that all key industries should be brought under the public sector.

It is of the opinion that basic consumer industries should be immediately nationalized to stabilize the prices of the consumer goods and to save the poor consumer from exploitation at the hands of the industrialists and the middleman.

The public sector industries should be established in such a way that the imbalance between different States is removed.

A planned effort to establish agro-industries in the rural areas should be made to relieve the growing population pressure in the urban areas. The industrial management should be democratized by enabling the workers to have a say in the management and by fair distribution of profits between the industrialists and the workers. The credit agencies, especially the nationalized banks should be directed to invest a fixed ratio of their deposits in the rural areas. Every industrial unit beyond worth one crore assets should be brought under the public sector. The Akali Dal stands for progressive nationalization of Transport.

The Punjab Sector units should be fully autonomous and manned by competent young executive drawn from a central pool of talent.

Economic Policy

The Shiromani Akali Dal demands that the whole tax structure be revised in such a way that the evasion of taxes and the flow of black money is completely eradicated. It stands for a simple and straight forward system of taxation. The present infrastructure of taxation weighs heavily against the poor and enables the rich to by pass it. The party stands for a more realistic policy in this respect so that the black money running a parallel economy may be usefully employed.

Workers, Middle Class Employees And Agricultural Labour

For their benefits the Shiromani Akali Dal would try its best:

1. To fix need-based wages for industrial workers.
2. To bring progressive improvement in the standard of living of government employees.
3. To re-assess the minimum wages of agricultural labour and to standard of living for them.
4. To take necessary steps to provide roofed accommodation for standard of living for them.
5. To take necessary steps to provide roofed accommodation for the rural and urban poor.

Unemployment

The Shiromani Akali Dal stands for full employment in the country. For such a purpose it is of the firm opinion that the Government must provide immediate employment to the educated and trained persons, otherwise reasonable unemployment allowance should be paid to them. This amount should be shared by the centre and the state government. The minimum rates of such an allowance should be as under :

1. Matric and/or trained hands Rs. 50 per month
2. B.A. Rs. 75 per month
3. M.A. Rs. 100 per month
4. Engineers and Doctors Rs. 150 per month
5. Other trained labour Rs. 50 per month

All persons above the age of 65 should be given old age pension.

Weaker Section And Backward Classes

The Shiromani Akali Dal shall try to improve the economic conditions of the backward classes and weaker sections of Society by extending them facilities for education, employment and other concessions, to enable them to come at par with other sections of society. Foodgrains at cheaper rates would be made available to them.

Educational And Cultural

The Shiromani Akali Dal aims at grooming the Sikhs into a strong and sturdy Nation highly educated, fully aware of its fundamental rights, very well versed in various arts and ever ready to honour the more outstanding of its sons. For such a purpose :

1. The Shiromani Akali Dal regards the educationists, scientists, philosophers, poets, writers and artists of the Sikh Nation as its most prized asset.
2. The Shiromani Akali Dal stands for compulsory and free education up to matric standard.
3. To check the growing rate of unemployment, Shiromani Akali Dal would try to introduce such

courses of study as would enable their students to get immediate employment on completion of a course.

4. The Shiromani Akali Dal shall make arrangements for the education of the rural and weaker classes and would also make provision for the higher education of the more promising students among them.
5. Punjabi would be a compulsory subject for all students upto the matric standard.
6. Special attention would be paid to the science and technical fields of education, with particular emphasis on the study of nuclear physics and space science in the universities.
7. The Shiromani Akali Dal shall try to improve the standard of games and bring them on level with international standards.

Dated : 1.8.1977 Sd/-

Giani Ajmer Singh
Secretary, Shiromani Akali Dal

Source : Verinder Grover, (Ed.) *The Story of Punjab : Yesterday and Today*, Vol. III. Deep and Deep Publications, New Delhi, 1995

Appendix -B

Rajiv Gandhi-Longowal Accord

24 July 1985

1. Compensation to innocent persons killed.

   1.1 Along with ex-gratia payment to those innocent killed in agitation or any actions after 1.8.1982 compensation for property damaged will also be paid.

2. Army requirement.

   2.1 All citizens of the country have the right to enroll in the army and merit will remain the criterion for selection.

3. Enquiry into November incidents.

   3.1 The jurisdiction of Mr. Justice Ranganath Mishra Commission enquiring into the November riots of Delhi would be extended to cover the disturbances at Bokaro and Kanpur also.

4. Rehabilitation of those discharged from the army.

   4.1 For all those discharged, efforts will be made to rehabilitate and provide gainful employment.

5. All-India Gurudwara Act.

   5.1 The Government of India agrees to consider the formulation of an All-India Government Bill. Legislation will be brought forward for this purpose in consultation with Shiromani Akali Dal, others concerned and after fulfilling all relevant constitutional requirements.

6. Disposal of pending cases.

6.1 The notifications applying the Armed forces Special Powers Act, Punjab will be withdrawn.

Existing special courts will try only cases relating to the following types of offences :

(A) Waging war

(B) Hijacking.

6.2 All other cases will be transferred to ordinary courts and enabling legislation if needed will be brought forward in this session of Parliament.

7. Territorial claims

7.1 The capital project area of Chandigarh will go to Punjab.

Some adjoining areas which were previously part of Hindi or the Punjabi regions were included in the Union territory. With the capital region going to Punjab the areas which were added to the Union territory from the Punjabi region of the erstwhile state of Punjab will be transferred to Punjab and those from Hindi region to Haryana. The entire Sukhna Lake will be kept as part of the Chandigarh and will thus go to Punjab.

7.2 It had always been maintained by Mrs. Indira Gandhi that when Chandigarh is to go to Punjab some Hindi-speaking terrritories in Punjab will go to Haryana. A commision will be constituted to determine the specific Hindi-speaking areas of Punjab which should go to Haryana, in lieu of Chandigarh.

The principle of continunity and linguistic affinity with a village as a unity will be the basis of such determination.

The Commision will be required to give its findings by December 31, 1985 and these will be binding on both sides.

The work of the Commision will be limited to this aspect and will be distinct from the general boundary claims which the other commision referred to in Para 7.4 will handle.

7.3 The actual transfer of Chandigarh to Punjab and areas in lieu therefore to Haryana will take place simultaneously on January 26, 1986.

7.4 There are other claims and counter-claims for readjustment of daries (territories). The government will appoint (in addition to) the existing Punjab-Haryana boundary (commision) another commision to consider these matters and give its findings. Such findings will be binding on the concerned states. The terms of reference will be based on a village as a unit, linguistic affinity and contiguity.

8. Centre-State relations

8.1 Shiromani Akali Dal states that the Anandpur Sahib resolution is entirely within the framework of the Indian Constitution, that it attempts to define the concept of Centre-State relations in a manner which may bring out the true federal characteristics of our unitary constitutions, and that the purpose of the resolution is to provide greater autonomy, to the state with a view to strengthening the unity and integrity of the country, since unity in diversity forms the corner-stone of our national entity.

8.2 In view of the above, the Anandpur Sahib resolution insofar as it deals with the Centre-State relations, stands to the Sarkaria Commision.

9. Sharing of rivers waters.

9.1 The farmers of Punjab, Haryana and Rajasthan will continue to get water not less than what they are using from the Ravi-Beas system as on 1.7.1985. Water used for consumptive purposes will also remain unaffected. Quantum of usage claimed shall be verified by the tribunal referred to in para 9.2 below.

9.2 The claims of Punjab and Haryana regarding the shares in their remaining waters will be referred or adjudication to a tribunal to be presided over by a Supreme Court Judge. The decision of this tribunal will be rendered within six months and would be binding on both parties. All legal and constitutional steps required in this respect be taken expeditiously.

9.3 The construction of the SYL canal shall continue. The canal shall be completed by August 15, 1986.

10. Representation of minorities.

10.1 Existing instructions regarding protection of interests of minorities will be recirculated to the State Chief Ministers, (PM will write to all Chief Ministers).

11. Promotion of Punjabi language.

11.1 The Central Government may take some steps for the promotion of the Punjabi language.

This settlement brings to an end a period of confrontation and ushers in an era of amity, goodwill and cooperation, which will promote and strengthen the unity and integrity of India.

Source : Verinder Grover, (Ed.) *The Story of Punjab : Yesterday and Today*, Vol. III. Deep and Deep Publications, New Delhi, 1995

Bibliography

BOOKS

Ahluwalia, M.L. *Land Marks in Sikh History : A Fully Researched and Documented History (1699-1947)*, Ashoka International Publishers, New Delhi, 1996.

Alaxender Yonah and Semmour Maxwall, *Terrorism : Interdisciplinary Perspective*, MacGraw-Hill Book Company Ltd., U.S.A.

Brar, Lt. Gen. K.S., *Operation Blue Star : The True Story*, UBS Publishers and Distributors Ltd., New Delhi,1993.

Brass, Paul R., *Language, Religion and Politics in North India*, Vikas Publishing House, New Delhi, 1975.

Deng, Satyapal, *Genesis of Terrorism in Punjab*, Patriot Publication, New Delhi, 1988.

Gaur, Madan, *Pointers in Punjab*, Press and P.R. Service Publication, 1985.

Grover, Verinder (Ed.), *The Story of Punjab : Yesterday and Today*, vol. I, II and III, Deep and Deep Publications, New Delhi,1995.

Gulterdge, William, (Ed.) *The New Terrorism*, Monsel Publication Ltd., London, 1986.

Gurr, Robert Ted, *Why Men Rebel*, Princeton University Press, Princeton, New Jersey, 1971.

India, *White Paper on the Punjab Agitation*, Government of India, New Delhi, 1984.

Jeffery, Robin, *What is Happening to India? : Punjab, Ethnic Conflict, Mrs. Gandhi's Death and the Test for Federalism*, Macmillan, Zasingstoke, 1986.

Jenkins, Brian, *'International Terrorism : Trends and Potentialities'*, *Rand Corp*, Santamonica, California, 1977.

Kaur, Amarjit et al, *The Punjab Story*, Roli Book Internationl, New Delhi, 1984.

Kissinger, Henry A. (Ed.) *Problems of National Security*, Fredrick A. Praeger, USA, 1965.

Masood, Maqsood Ahmad and Peter Stockdale, *The Khalistan Riddle*, Modern Book Depot, AAB PARA, Islamabad, Pakistan, 1988.

Naunihal Singh, *The World of Terrorism*, South Asia Publishers, New Delhi, 1989.

Nayar, Baldev Raj, *Minority Politics in the Punjab*. Princeton, 1966.

Nayar, Kuldip and Khushwant Singh, *Tragedy of Punjab : Operation Blue Star and After*, Vision Books New Delhi, 1988.

Parmanand, *Political Development in South Asia*, Sterling Publishers P. Ltd., New Delhi, 1988.

Samiuddin, Abida, *Punjab Crisis : Challenges and Response*, Mittal Publication, New Delhi, 1985.

Saxena, K.S. and Anil Gupta, *Indian Democracy : Recent Trends and Issues*, Amol Publications, Delhi-51. 1985.

Saksena, N.S., *Terrorism, History and Facets*, Abhinav Publication, New Delhi, 1985.

Segar, Karl A, *The Anti-Terrorism Handbook*, Lancer International, New Delhi, 1990.

Shaileshwar, Nath, *Terrorism in India*, National Publishing House Delhi, 1980.

Shakir, Moin, *Politics of Minorities*, Ajanta Publication, Delhi, 1986.

Sharma, D.P., *The Punjab Story : A Decade of Turmoil*, APH Publishing Corporation, New Delhi, 1996.

Sharma, D.P., *Countering Terrorism*, Lancers Book, New Delhi 1992.

Singh, Amrik, *Punjab in Indian Politics : Issues and Trends*, Oriental University Press, Delhi, 1986.

Singh, Khushwant, *How the Sikhs Lost Their Kingdom*, UBS Publishers and Distributors Ltd., New Delhi, 1996.

Singh, Khushwant, *My Bleeding Punjab*, UBS Publishers and Distributors Ltd., New Delhi 1992.

Singh, Khushwant, '*A History of the Sikhs, 1839-1964*, Vol. I and II, Princeton University Press, 1966.

Singh, Mohinder, *The Akali Struggle : A Retrospect*, Atlantic Publishers and Distributors, New Delhi, 1989.

Singh, Shailendra, *Khalistan : An Academic Analysis*, Amar Prakashan, New Delhi, 1982.

Sinha, Sachchidanand, et al., *Action in Punjab : Prelude and Aftermath*, Samta Era Publication, New Delhi, 1984.

Sonal, Capt. Ashish, *Terrorism, and Insurgency in India : A Study of the Human Element*, Lancers Publishers Pvt. Ltd., New Delhi, 1994.

Taneja, K.L., *Sikh Politics (1920-1940)*, Vishal Publication, Kurushetra, 1984.

Tiwari, S.C., *Terrorism in India*, South Asia Publication, New Delhi, 1990.

Wood, John R. (Ed.) *State Politics in Contemporary India : Crisis or Continuity*, Westview Press, Boulder, 1984.

ARTICLES

Bohannan, Charles T.R., 'Anti-Guerrilla Operations', *The Annals*, vol. 341, May 1962.

Gujaral, I.K., 'The Sequence', *Seminar*, February 1984.

IDR Research Team, 'Punjab : Profile of a Terrorist Movement', *Indian Defence Review*, vol. II, July 1987.

Kathpalia, P.N., ' Counter Measures Against Terrorism', *Indian Defence Review* Vol. II, No.2, July 1987.

Kothari, Rajni and Giri Deshingkar, ' Punjab : The Longer View' *Illustrated Weekly of India*, July, 1984.

Majeed, Akhtar, 'Tackling International Terrorism', *Strategic Studies Journal*, vol. 1 No. 1, 1988.

O'Brian, Conor Cruise, 'Holy War Against India', *Mainstream* September, 1988.

Puri, H.K., 'Akali-Agitation : An Analysis of Socio-Economic Basis of Protest', *Economic and Political Weekly*, January,1983.

Rana, Sangram Singh, 'Punjab Problem : A Study of Resultant Forces', *Asian Profile* l, Vol. XII, No.I', February, 1984.

Saksena, N.S., 'Roots of Terrorism in Punjab', *Times of India*, 6 December, 1983.

Saksena, N.S., 'Dangerous Illusion About Terrorism', *Times of India*, 10 April, 1984.

Singh B.D., 'Punjab Problem : A Perspective', *Mainstream*, Vol. XXII, No. 3,5 May, 1984.

Singh B.D., 'Punjab : Lessons and Prospects', Mainstream, Vol. XXII, No. 43,23 June, 1984.

Singh, Gopal, 'Socio-economic Bases of Punjab Crisis', *Economic and Political Weekly*, January 1984.

Singh, Gopal, 'Terrorism in Punjab : Supposed Modus Operandi and Objectives, *Mainstream*, 24 July, 1988.

Singh, Gurharpal, 'Understanding the Punjab Problem', *Asian Survey*, December, 1987.

Singh, Shaukin, 'War of Attrition', *Link* vol. XXVI, No. 52, 29 July, 1984.

Singh, Sukhjit, 'The Punjab : 1993', *Indian Defence Review*, Vol, 8, No.3, July 1993.

Subrahmanyam, K., 'Terrorism; *Strategic Analysis* , vol. 9, No.4, 1985.

Subrahmanyam, K., `Terrorism to the Forefront of the Stage', *Strategic Analysis*, vol. 10, No.3, 1986.

Swarup, Ram, 'Happenings in Punjab : A Form of Guerrila Warfare', *Times of India*, 21 April, 1984.

Swarup, Ram., 'Akali Politics and Terrorism', *Times of India*, 30 July 1984.

Thaper, K.S., 'Akali Communalism : Genesis and Implications', *Mainstream*, vol.21, No. 24, February 12, 1982.

Index